GOD AND ME

GOD AND ME

*Reflections on Relationship,
Fruitfulness and the Kingdom*

MIKE ENDICOTT

Order of Jacob's Well Trust

Copyright © Order of Jacob's Well Trust 2015
All rights reserved.

First published 2014
No part of this publication may be reproduced or transmitted in any
form or by any means, electronic or mechanical, including photocopy,
recording or any information storage and retrieval system, without
permission in writing from the publisher.

Published in Great Britain by
The Order of Jacob's Well Trust
Forge House, Clomendy Rd, Old Cwmbran, Wales NP44 3LS UK
www.jacobswell.org.uk
www.simplyhealing.org

Scripture marked "NIV":
Scripture taken from the Holy Bible, New International Version®.
Copyright © 1979, 1984 Biblica, Inc.
Used by permission of Hodder & Stoughton Publishers,
an Hachette UK company.
All rights reserved.
"NIV" is a registered trademark of Biblica.
UK trademark number 1448790.

USA acknowledgement
Scriptures marked "NIV":
Scripture taken from the HOLY BIBLE, NEW INTERNATIONAL
VERSION®. NIV®. Copyright © 1973, 1978, 1984 by International
Bible Society. Used by permission of Zondervan.
All rights reserved worldwide.

Scripture marked "AMP"
Scripture quotations taken from the Amplified® Bible,
Copyright © 1954, 1958, 1962, 1964, 1965, 1987 by
The Lockman Foundation
Used by permission. (www.Lockman.org)

ISBN 978-1508831679

Printed by CreateSpace

Contents

	ACKNOWLEDGEMENTS	9
1.	LOOKING AROUND CHURCH AND WORLD	11
2.	WALKING TOGETHER	25
3.	OUR ADOPTION	37
4.	A MORE WORTHY PRIESTHOOD	49
5.	HIS KINGDOM, OUR KINGDOM	57
6.	TRUSTING THE LORD	65
7.	RESTING IN THE KINGDOM	77
8.	HIDING IN HIM	87
9.	NETWORKING WITH GOD	97
	SUMMARY	115

As always, I ask the reader to compare everything I say or write with what is written in the Bible and, if at any point a conflict is found, always to rely upon the clear teaching of scripture.

Mike Endicott

ACKNOWLEDGEMENTS

My greatest thanks to Helen Dowdell and to Revd Sam Caton for the countless hours they have devoted to our cause of finding a way to seek first the kingdom of God and his righteousness.

Their devotion to prayer, to the study of the scriptures and to their straightforward expressions of truths discovered have greatly opened all our hearts to the reality of dying to self, that our lives can now be hidden with Christ in God.

1

LOOKING AROUND CHURCH AND WORLD

WHO'S RUNNING THE WORLD?
A few minutes thought leads us too easily to a place of complaining about any of the bigger issues of life. Let's take a snapshot of certain aspects of living in our world today, in the twenty-first century.

It seems that our lives as ordinary people are ruled by two major systems: politics and economics. In the western hemisphere we go on to use these two systems to maintain our politically induced organisations and our democracies. We spend a great deal of military and political and diplomatic effort trying to uphold other democracies, and in persuading other types of political society to change to democracy. It's what we think is best for them.

These major ruling systems are there for our benefit, to improve our lifestyles and, in the main, to do it by improving our rate of consumption. But look again at the tenth commandment,

> "You shall not covet your neighbour's house. You shall not covet your neighbour's wife, or his male or female servant, his ox or donkey, or anything that belongs to your neighbour."
>
> *Exodus 20:17* (NIV)

And yet we still tend to believe that unconditional

happiness will almost certainly come our way through this insatiable appetite for consuming but, no matter how much it manages to stuff its tummy, we are still left psychologically like Oliver Twist in the poorhouse, holding up an empty bowl and begging, "I want some more!"

It might well be, from the beginning, that our constant longing for the 'good' society contains in its nature a major flaw; a hidden and built-in violation of the Tenth Commandment — You shall not covet your neighbour's goods.

Unhappily these major systems have proved well enough that they do not work. We fight tooth and nail to retain them as our controlling factors, having a great fear of allowing any change to take place in that which we know and love, even though as systems they prove unreliable.

Evidence of their failure can be regularly and clearly seen throughout history and in particular in recent times.

POLITICS

The instability of society in many African, Middle Eastern and Asian countries in various ways points to a disastrous lack of concrete substance in our ideas of how we should carry out politics.

We rely both on politics and diplomacy to manage our world and yet some of us have been at war with others of us for centuries, the ultimate crime of humanity those systems are supposed to prevent from happening.

ECONOMICS

This century has been plagued by certain activities in the banking sector which have led to agonising worldwide depression and loss of living standards. Five major countries in Europe have struggle to survive financially and have had to be rescued by the others around them from the pit in which they found themselves, for other reasons, as well as because of banking issues.

DEMOCRACY
Of course we can all find things we dislike about dictatorships, autocracies, rule by religion etc. But the democracy in which we live is supposed to be the rule of the majority view. Observers living in democracies will be well aware that their own form of democracy is growing more and more towards being ruled not by the majority but by minority views, activities and opinions.

THE CHURCH
These major systems, politics and economics as we know them, are unsound. Even the structure of the church is shattering apart around us. We now have more Christian denominations in our dwindling church than she has ever had in her entire history!

And within the Christian church there have developed, over the centuries, a huge range of differing ideas about the nature of God and his kingdom. These different views are not credited as being heretical in any way, as we seem to want to allow and accommodate all minority views.

But logic dictates that all views other than the truth must be heretical by definition. We overcome this understanding by claiming that man cannot understand God anyway, and therefore any individual opinion is, and must surely be, an acceptable although small part of the whole.

OUR SOLUTION
When things appear to go very wrong around the world the Christian response is to pray. Many Christians are involved in the realms of intercession, spiritual warfare, spiritual mapping, healing ministry of all shapes and kinds, geographical deliverance, etc., all of which leads to untouched secrets of disappointment in many hearts.

The general nature of such prayer is to invite God to step down from the heavenlies into our mess, straighten out the effects of the mess we have made and then bless us to move on along the same messy way as before. But if we truly lived within the boundaries of the kingdom of God, instead of making our way in the kingdom of self, if we really loved God as we should, then we would not be forever trying different albeit prayerful ways of pulling God down from heaven into our mess; in truth we would more naturally be doing the opposite. We would be forever holding our own hearts up into the heavenly realms, up to the throne of the Most High, begging God to remould our hearts and wills to fit his will much better.

In the story of the prodigal son, the boy concerned climbed out of his pigsty and went back to his father, he did not cry out for his father to bring him some more food and money while he continued the un-kingdom life he was leading in that far off country. Romans 12:1, 2 (NIV) says,

> Therefore, I urge you, brothers and sisters, in view of God's mercy, to offer your bodies as a living sacrifice, holy and pleasing to God—this is your true and proper worship. Do not conform to the pattern of this world, but be transformed by the renewing of your mind. Then you will be able to test and approve what God's will is—his good, pleasing and perfect will."

To know God's will, to live within his will, to work with him, to know him better, we must do what those verses say. We must move towards the kingdom of God where the mind of Christ dictates all politics and economics. If we did this we would be engaging ourselves in true and proper worship. The Bible calls us to not 'conform to the pattern of this world', its politics, its economic systems, its relentless search for the elevation of self.

DIVINE ADVICE

Jesus says to us in Matthew 6:33 (NIV), "But seek first his kingdom and his righteousness, and all these things will be given to you as well."

KINGDOM OF GOD?
Another system for running both church and world? "No chance!" we cry, "The world doesn't want to go to church any more!" Maybe not, but this little book is designed to help the reader find their own place, on the way towards living in the kingdom of God. If then their light is set on a hill where everyone can see it, then someone else may follow them.

HOW DID THIS HAPPEN?
Adam and Eve were tempted by the serpent to eat a fruit which, says the Bible, had two main attractions: they saw that it was tasty and it was good for gaining wisdom. And that's our problem: human wisdom. The world's political and economic systems, and we may add the church's ecclesiastical structure, are things run by *man's* wisdom. We may wish to defend them on practical or even on spiritual grounds but we should be aware of fighting to maintain the status quo when it might be in the wrong kingdom.

This is not God's wisdom (which the Genesis creation story refers to) but mankind's wisdom. If Adam and Eve could acquire a dose of their own wisdom for themselves then they would not have to refer and defer to God in all matters. They would be able to make up their own minds and do what they themselves thought would be best. They could use their own mind instead of God's to make their decisions. This is rule not by God's wisdom but by ours.

In black and white, this leads to there now being two kingdoms: God's and ours, one is ruled by God in his wisdom and the other is ruled by self with our own wisdom.

WHERE ARE WE NOW?
Our two major systems, politics and economics, are both firmly rooted in the kingdom of self. Their driving forces are self-motivated. They feed self-advancement, self-satisfaction, self-importance, self-centredness, self-worth, self-provision.

WHO IS GOD?

The God of the kingdom of God is God. The god of the kingdom of self is self. These two cannot be reconciled without the Cross of Christ. They are, and will always be, at loggerheads with each other. Do we have the humility to ask of ourselves, "Which is our real god – the Almighty or self?

There are two kingdoms, God's and self's, the kingdoms of darkness and light. We, all of us, live quite naturally in the kingdom of self, the kingdom of darkness. Because of the work of Christ on the Cross we are now free to travel from the kingdom of darkness into the kingdom of light.

Convincing ourselves that we have already made that journey leads to a closing of our eyes to Jesus' injunction to "Be holy as I am holy". Here is one of those commands again, "Seek first the kingdom of God and his righteousness...." Here is the hammer blow against Christian complacency in such matters. Here, too, is the athlete's starting gun that should begin to propel us down the track, down the journey out of the self-kingdom managed by our own wisdom, and to seek the kingdom of God and his righteousness. And here God calls us to live in his righteousness, not our innate goodness.

> "For I tell you that unless your righteousness surpasses that of the Pharisees and the teachers of the law, you will certainly not enter the kingdom of heaven."
>
> *Matthew 5:20* (NIV)

> "Not everyone who says to me, 'Lord, Lord,' will enter the kingdom of heaven, but only the one who does the will of my Father who is in heaven. Many will say to me on that day, 'Lord, Lord, did we not prophesy in your name and in your name drive out demons and in your name perform many miracles?' Then I will tell them plainly, 'I never knew you. Away from me, you evildoers!'"
>
> *Matthew 7:21–23* (NIV)

So God is not particularly seeking those who can perform spiritually, even though they might do so out of feelings of love for him. For God says,

"If you love me, keep my commands" *John 14:15* (NIV).

He is seeking our obedience.

A MORE GODLY CHURCH
It is very encouraging sometimes to read through the Acts of the Apostles, but to do it from a few paces back. It is all revealed truth but an overview helps us to see, appreciate and understand individual phrases and verses.

NATURAL AND EASY
Standing back a little, we can see the real picture of what is going on within its pages. Time and again we can find, by treating the book this way, that miracle working must have been thought about in those days as being quite natural, and relatively easy to do. So what was it like then, in New Testament times? What was it like to see miracles flourishing in the everyday early church? What was the promise on the horizon? Compared with the modern church's ministry to the sick and the injured, church life in those days must have been quite breathtaking!

BREATHTAKING MISSION
We can see this when Paul confirmed in writing to the Corinthians that, when he was with them, he did things that marked an apostle – signs, wonders and miracles, and these things were done among them with great perseverance. Such signs were obviously expected of an apostle, but perhaps not so much today. Why not?

We can move on through the pages of the New Testament

and watch in our mind's eye the whole assembly growing quiet as they listen enthralled to Barnabas and Paul telling them about the miraculous signs and wonders God had done through them while on mission among the Gentiles.

We can read of Peter describing to his critics the healing of a disabled beggar as 'an act of kindness'. We might ourselves consider describing the helping of an old person across the street or perhaps a small gift to charity as an everyday sort of act of kindness, but in those days the term was used to describe everyday miracle-working. They must have found it a lot easier!

We can follow Peter travelling about the country, visiting the saints in a place called Lydda. He comes across a man there called Aeneas, who has been bedridden for eight years. We can read of Peter saying to him, "Aeneas, Jesus Christ heals you. Get up and tidy up your mat."

The man gets up immediately and all the people living locally who have seen it turn to the Lord. They have seen the living God working in their midst and the experience contributes hugely to their conversion.

In those exciting early days the apostles performed many miraculous signs and wonders among the people, and we can read in the New Testament how more and more men and women believed in the Lord and were added to their number as a result. We can see people bringing the sick into the streets and laying them on beds and mats, in the hope that at least Peter's shadow would fall across some of them as he walked past them, and all of them were healed. That is breathtaking!

NOT US, SURELY!

But before we begin to graciously excuse ourselves from this scene, before we put distance between ourselves and those events by supposing that only Jesus' own appointed and anointed apostles can perform miracles like this, we find Deacon Stephen, a man full of God's grace and power, doing great wonders and miraculous signs among the people. And then there is Deacon Philip, who goes down to a city in Samaria and proclaims the Christ there. When the crowds heard him speak, and watched the miraculous things he was doing, they all sat up and paid attention to what he was up to . The miracles God was working through him were themselves the perfect proof of what he was talking about.

And it goes on! The flow of God's grace and power is not, as some may believe today, limited to those officially ordained or appointed or anointed in the church. Ordinary everyday people like us were greatly used in the working of miracles. These ordinary men and women, Jesus' disciples, went out and preached everywhere, and the Lord worked with them and confirmed his word by the signs that accompanied it. Oh, if only that were true today! If only we could convince our congregations that they can have the power of the message of the cross on their lips!

We have the power to evangelise the world, someone once said, but they are asleep in the pews!

Do we actually fear to put our money where our mouths are? We want our congregations to be out there, witnessing to the kingdom, but they might have to face all sorts of questions they might not know the answers to so, generally speaking today, they won't go there.

ANSWERS IN ADVANCE?
Many church leaders like to maintain the church's religious knowledge base inside themselves, so the church rarely provides occasions for its people to study kingdom issues. Could this be because they don't know them either? How many kingdom secrets have been lost down the centuries?

So we find, looking back, a picture of an enthusiastic and powerful church family, with an effective family ministry. They worshipped Jesus Christ, who died on the cross to pay the price of their sins and was raised from the dead, who is now alive and reigns and is their Saviour, Healer and Lord.

HOW DID THEY OPERATE?
They proclaimed the good news of the message of the cross, the gospel of righteousness — his righteousness instead of our own. And they knew that they were being saved and healed as they continued in faith, and were being sanctified as they went on being filled with the Holy Spirit, abiding in Jesus and walking his way in obedience and faith, learning to overcome in this world.

They also demonstrated that the Lord's compassionate heart was still for healing the sick and the injured of this world! They all knew what to do. It was a lot of what Christians did. Many saw and many listened and many came to Christ – and it often seems, somehow, that we have lost it!

ARE WE NOTICED NOWADAYS?
Precious few outsiders notice the church much any more. Can we go back to how it used to be? Well, what does Jesus claim? Unless we approach him with a trusting attitude like that of little children we are going to miss it. How exciting! We must be prepared to go on a childlike adventure again, and look at where it takes us.

INTO THE UNKNOWN
We seem sometimes to know very little of kingdom dynamics after two thousand years of spiritual and theological development. If we were well acquainted with the kingdom of God, and his righteousness, then we would all be workers of miracles like our spiritual forefathers. The proof is in the pudding, and allowing our healing prayer ministry to go on drifting further and further away from the purity of its original form is killing off our involvement in fruit production.

JUST IMAGINE!

Would it not be marvellous if the local non-believers could say to each other: 'Let's go up to that church where people get healed!'

Unbelievers really care very little about what we believe. We can be 'nice' at church outreach events but it doesn't help that much. Nor does being an example of wholesome living standards stand out much. There are plenty of folk living like that out there. There are more 'nice' people outside the church than there are inside it!

Power is the thing that unbelievers are looking for today, and they are not, in the main, listening to our attempts at preaching. They have plenty of problems and not enough solutions.

They are sick. They are hooked on alcohol and drugs. Their relationships are tearing them apart. It's a mess out there.

TIMING

Never before has the field been so ready for harvest, so ripe for the display of God's kingdom grace. The enemy, whether we prefer to call it the Fall or self or Satan's demonic hordes and influences, has turned the lives of too many unbelievers upside down to such an extent that many have no idea where to go or what to do to get their lives put back together again.

They really care very little if we Christians speak in tongues or dance in the aisles or stand up straight and sing out of a hymnal. But if only we, the people of God, had the ministry to get their bodies healed and their lives straightened out as would have happened in the early church, they would come to wherever we are. Not only that, but they might start listening to what we have to say.

DOES GOD WANT SUCH A THING?

God wants his church to have the same reputation today that Jesus had during his earthly ministry. Surely, he wants people to say the same sort of things about us that they must have said to each other about those first-generation disciples. They would have noticed that the power of God was at work in believers.

To the general public, the gospel without power does not sound particularly like good news to them. We already-converted ones know full well that it is, because it brings salvation, but it doesn't look like that to outsiders. To a huge number of them, love without power is only a pipe dream and love mixed with power is what justice is made up of.

And given the seemingly random effects of the Fall, they have great needs in their minds and their bodies. If the only thing we Christians have to give folk is a new set of rules to live by and a new set of standards to live up to, teaching them a mode of life without really changing their lives, what good have we done for them? If we are not careful then we have merely bound them up with yet another set of rules.

True disciples will be sharing in the compassion of Jesus for people, and longing to see them gather around him. We can never say to anyone that our conversion is complete until it has filled us with an overwhelming awareness of responsibility both for rescuing the downtrodden and fulfilling the great commission.

Someone once commented that the church exists for those outside itself. It also exists to worship God, but there is always a real danger that we may turn into a little huddle of pious people, shutting our doors against the world, connoisseurs of liturgy, lost in prayer and praise, congratulating each other on the excellence of our Christian experience.

If only we were willing to take a risk and deal with the sick and downtrodden in the way that Jesus taught and practised, then we would be doing again an important part of what God sent us to do. And as people watch what we do, they would listen to what we have to say. Then it is possible they might begin to care about what we believe, and hear and respond to the words of eternal life, the word of truth.

ARE WE OK?
We must have a lively, active ministry which comes up with the goods! Our ministry has to do what it says on the tin, as they say. People today are not so excited by religious theories as we might have been a few hundred years ago. Today's worldly general public are not overawed and duped by high ritual or by any practices at all that don't come up with significant and measurable results. That's the way the world is.

We need to see a ministry with tangible consequences, as we see in the earthly ministry of Jesus and the apostles. We need something that works and, it would appear to the simple childlike mind that the early church, men and women, had just that!

MODELLING OURSELVES
Christians involved in prayer for others, if we are to get back to being true student disciples in this matter, must show everyone else that we take the New Testament to be the measure of our ministry. If we don't actively model the original revelation of Jesus and his apostles in healing ministry, then we might be vulnerable, in all humility, to teaching and demonstrating our own ideas, theological traditions and theories. Not only have these shown themselves to contain opportunities for misuse and abuse, they can also be extremely hurtful and often downright wrong.

Many of our ministry practices, in the twenty-first century, are not reflecting the teaching and practice of Jesus and his apostles. Jesus did not demonstrate some of the ideas and practices that many of us follow to this day. He did not commission any of his original followers to do a lot of them, either.

That does not invalidate or condemn what many of us are doing, and still do to this day. It simply raises an interesting question: if we were to stick to a 'replica' ministry, would we then see results, the sick healed and God glorified in New Testament proportions? Because, if so, then perhaps people will see his glory and listen to our message and come into the fellowship of the kingdom of God.

A LIFE IN THE KINGDOM

The way forward is not so difficult, and the yoke of Christ is a light one. This book sets out to demonstrate that God requires us to have a working relationship with him through Jesus Christ, a 'walking together'.

The more we work with this arrangement the deeper grows our relationship with him. The deeper the relationship the more we are governed by the 'mind of Christ'.

The more we are governed by his thinking the more we are in harmony with him, the more our lives are filled with his peace and the easier the fruit will grow on the vine!

2

WALKING TOGETHER

A SUGGESTED REBUILD

As so many parts of the Christian Church worldwide decline numerically, some say gently, some say disastrously —thousands of thinking members at every ecclesiastical level are continuously devising a kaleidoscopic variety of programmes of recovery — each one of which, it is often suggested, contains their particular idea of the true seed of church membership revival. And yet, despite all our efforts, the decline continues remorselessly.

The encouragement to a closer walk with him, as expressed in this little book, is not suggesting another method of rejuvenation as yet untried. It is, however, a suggestion to the reader which may help spiritually to rebuild and refurbish both themselves and the organisation.

It would most certainly do two other things as well; it would bring the church into much greater harmony with God, and it would bring great glory to him. If parts of the organisation fade away in the due course of time, at least the church will have been obedient to our calling, to be in harmony with God.

THE SANDWICH MAKER

Walking together with God in his kingdom work is a very simple idea and it goes like this:

On his way back to heaven Jesus offered his disciples a 'sandwich'. We properly call that sandwich 'The Great

Commission'. Actually 'offer' might not be a good word to use in this context as it implies something that might be optional. Far from being an option for Christians, the Commission sandwich idea contains a divine command to all of us to 'eat' it, to swallow the idea, to take it on board in our daily lives.

WHY CALL IT A 'SANDWICH'?

The Commission is a set of instructions describing a closer relationship in kingdom work. It is put together in three layers: a slice of bread (think Jesus) on top and another slice underneath (think Jesus again). You and I are the juicy filling in the middle!

This is an analogous description of the God-designed, God-required relationship in working together between us and himself. Here it is in Matthew 28:18 – 20 (NIV),

God's role in this kingdom work
"All authority in heaven and on earth has been given to me.

Our role in this kingdom work
"Therefore go and make disciples of all nations, baptizing them in the name of the Father and of the Son and of the Holy Spirit, and teaching them to obey everything I have commanded you."

God's role in this kingdom work
"And surely I am with you always, to the very end of the age."

So working closer together works like this: he does his bit if we do our bit. He does what he wants to do – extend the kingdom, rebuild creation – and we, in this 'working together' arrangement, teach what he taught. We do indeed already have the revealed Word of God for this, but our role is to testify to it, to witness to the truth of Christ crucified and raised to life.

And faith comes by hearing so we are expected to make a noise about something!

HAS ANYONE TRIED IT?

Did anyone else do it this way? Did anyone else proclaim the kingdom of God, stand back and watch God go to work? Well, watch Moses and then Joshua, watch Elijah on Mount Carmel, watch Jesus in the Gospels, watch the 12 and the 72, watch Paul, Barney and Deacons Phil and Steve, watch the mission of the early church, and they are all doing it!

They are in no way leading with their own specialist skills or practices (as we might be inclined to do) nor relying on weighty intercession or the flow of sacramental benefits. They are instead doing what Jesus told them, teaching what Jesus taught them. And what was that?

PROCLAIMING CROSS AND KINGDOM

He proclaimed the good news of the kingdom of God. This is the divine deal — do that, and he does his role in this working together, exercising the authority and the will of God to restore the mess we have made of his creation. And just look at the bottom piece of bread! He is always here with us to do it, wherever we are and whatever we are faced with.

To put this in a simple nutshell, we proclaim cross and kingdom and God then gets to work and does the rebuilding. This closeness of working together is based on trust, as it would be if, for example, two people were working with one another to achieve a common aim.

WHAT POWER?

The power of God is in the message of the cross; we speak it out, faith expectancy rises and he can do his bit.

"For the message of the cross is foolishness to those

who are perishing, but to us who are being saved it is the power of God."

1 Corinthians 1:18 (NIV)

The message of the kingdom is the thing that contains the power of God. the Bible does not say that the power lies in our charismatic speaking capabilities or in our ecclesiastical rank or in our own gift of the gab. Neither is the message fouled in any way by our inability to say all the right things at the right time. No, the power is in the message itself!

LOSS OF FOCUS

Those who say, "But God is God! It's up to us to pray and then God will do as he likes!" have never tried to do this business the way that God required the church to do it! We pray for the manifestation of God's love and caring healing, but the words and works of the names listed earlier are not recorded praying this way. They proclaimed the good news of cross and kingdom and the sick got healed in droves. They did their bit, he did his bit, and the kingdom advanced.

> "And these signs will accompany those who believe: In my name they will drive out demons; they will speak in new tongues; they will pick up snakes with their hands; and when they drink deadly poison, it will not hurt them at all; they will place their hands on sick people, and they will get well."
>
> After the Lord Jesus had spoken to them, he was taken up into heaven and he sat at the right hand of God. Then the disciples went out and preached everywhere, and the Lord worked with them and confirmed his word by the signs that accompanied it."
>
> *Mark 16:17 – 20* (NIV)

That is a perfect working arrangement, God and his disciples working in tandem with each other! Here is the challenge and here is the fear that goes with it — most of the church doesn't know how to do this. We've forgotten how to proclaim the good news of cross and kingdom. We have forgotten how to work in harmony with God.

"Don't go there!" we tell ourselves, "The ice is very thin!" But it's so easy to learn. All we need to do is try!

The Good News of the Kingdom
And here it is in do-it-yourself easy steps:

• Step 1
Take on board that the kingdom of God (the kingdom of heaven; same meaning) is a place where man can live in complete harmony with God himself and with others. Harmony with the Creator was there before the Fall. In the future there will be a new heaven and a new earth and God is making a new people to populate the new realm to come.

• Step 2
Take on board that when God laid down the Genesis kingdom blueprint he looked it over and commented, "This is very good." And there was no cancer, no arthritis, no relationships breaking down, no grief, no sorrow, and no 'just about everything else' that prevents us leading that originally blueprinted abundant life.

• Step 3
We can all agree that it isn't like that for most of us nowadays. We live in a comparative mess!

• Step 4
Consider the arrival of the New Jerusalem in the last book in the Bible. No more sickness and no more tears. It is like Eden restored.

Easy conclusion: it started being fabulous. It will end being fabulous. In the middle of our history between these two it is a mess – it is a deep trough full of sickness and despair.

The overriding will of God is to get his people from Genesis to Revelation.

• Step 5
Of his grace and mercy, the Father has intimated that we don't have to wait that long. He has sent Jesus in advance of the final Day of Judgement.

When with us in flesh, Jesus only really did two things before he set off towards Jerusalem: he proclaimed and healed. He told folks about the kingdom and proved it to fit in with the Father's great desire. (see steps 1–4 above).

When training his disciples (you and me today) he instructed them to proclaim the kingdom and heal the sick. Healing is a part of the great commission.

• Step 6
This next bit is really interesting and quite contrary to a great deal of modern teaching; Jesus never said 'No'. In relation to healing he never said 'Wait'. He never said 'Maybe, maybe not'. He never said 'No, you're a sinner', or 'No, you are not spiritually worthy!' He never needed to discern the root cause of someone's problem or cut them off from inherited demons travelling down the generations. He never told a supplicant he would have to pray about their sickness to discover God's will for them; he must have known it already and just said 'Yes!'

In truth, concerning healing he only ever said, 'Yes', and then said he was only doing what he saw the Father doing. And God, as we all know, doesn't change!

"But as surely as God is faithful, our message to you is not "Yes" and "No."

For the Son of God, Jesus Christ, who was preached among you by me and Silas and Timothy, was not "Yes" and "No," but in him it has always been "Yes."

For no matter how many promises God has made, they are "Yes" in Christ. And so through him the "Amen" is spoken by us to the glory of God."

2 Corinthians 1:18 – 20 (NIV)

He healed everyone who asked him, never turning anyone away. And this attitude to our human disarray seems totally in line with the Father's will to restore the mess that has been made of this world by mankind.

• Step 7

The self-emptying cross is like an exclamation mark at the end of his earthly ministry. It locks open the door for grace to flow. It's a finished and a complete work. The gate is now open that leads up the old Eden road.

As with so much else in our Christian lives, acceptance comes first, followed by understanding, not the other way around! When we can accept these basic steps of belief we are half way home!

The modern Christian approach, however, is to live life to the full and then, when something goes wrong, try to devise some way of attracting God's attention and involving him in solving the problem.

But when we go to work in the morning we do not climb in the car and reach for the cell phone to call the broadcasting company to tell them that we are ready, they can start broadcasting! We do not say to them, "I'm ready to hear you, so please send me a radio programme!" Why not?

Because we know that the broadcasting company is putting out radio programmes 24/7.

It is not our problem to persuade the broadcasting company to broadcast, but it is our problem to receive the programme being broadcast. We need to switch on the radio!

It is not our problem to persuade God to show us some signs of his kingdom, our problem is receiving the blessings!

- And this is the big **Step 8**

We need to trust, somehow, that the work of Calvary is completed. It is finished. By his wounds we are healed. We need to be able to proclaim wholeheartedly that wholeness and healing belong to the supplicant because of what Jesus has done. That's the nature of the King and his kingdom. In doing this we proclaim the message of the cross. The river of grace is already flowing.

Two sides of a Coin

Healing and wholeness are part of the restoration to the Eden condition. And in redemption there is forgiveness. Healing and forgiveness flow together. Both come from God. They are the two sides of the same coin. We all know that forgiveness flows back into this world through the self-emptying cross but we have forgotten that healing and wholeness gifts are flowing along with it!

Could we bring ourselves to cease our incessant whining at God and shift gear into praise and thanksgiving for what he has already done? Then we would be proclaiming out loud the greatest thing he has done for us. What might that be? The cross. Psalm 50:23 (NIV) says this;

> He who sacrifices thank offerings honours me, and he prepares the way so that I may show him the salvation of God.

This means learning to say thank you, not necessarily for blessings as yet unseen but for what he has already done. He has been sacrificed for us so that there is now nothing that can come between us and God.

WATCHING JOSHUA

Joshua at the battle of Jericho is a supreme example of the way it is intended for us to see the kingdom advanced. He does it God's way. Joshua has come into the Promised Land and turned a corner only to run up against a walled city, set out to defend itself against him. Here's the story again:

> Now Jericho was tightly shut up because of the Israelites. No one went out and no one came in. Then the LORD said to Joshua, "See, I have delivered Jericho into your hands, along with its king and its fighting men. March around the city once with all the armed men. Do this for six days.
>
> "Have seven priests carry trumpets of rams' horns in front of the ark. On the seventh day, march around the city seven times, with the priests blowing the trumpets. When you hear them sound a long blast on the trumpets, have all the people give a loud shout; then the wall of the city will collapse and the people will go up, every man straight in."
>
> So Joshua son of Nun called the priests and said to them, "Take up the ark of the covenant of the LORD and have seven priests carry trumpets in front of it."
>
> And he ordered the people, "Advance! March around the city, with the armed guard going ahead of the ark of the LORD."
>
> When Joshua had spoken to the people, the seven priests carrying the seven trumpets before the LORD went forward, blowing their trumpets, and the ark of the LORD's covenant followed them.
>
> The armed guard marched ahead of the priests who blew the trumpets, and the rear guard followed the ark.

All this time the trumpets were sounding.

But Joshua had commanded the people, "Do not give a war cry, do not raise your voices, do not say a word until the day I tell you to shout. Then shout!"

So he had the ark of the Lord carried around the city, circling it once. Then the people returned to camp and spent the night there. Joshua got up early the next morning and the priests took up the ark of the Lord.

The seven priests carrying the seven trumpets went forward, marching before the ark of the Lord and blowing the trumpets. The armed men went ahead of them and the rear guard followed the ark of the Lord, while the trumpets kept sounding.

So on the second day they marched around the city once and returned to the camp. They did this for six days.

On the seventh day, they got up at daybreak and marched around the city seven times in the same manner, except that on that day they circled the city seven times.

The seventh time around, when the priests sounded the trumpet blast, Joshua commanded the people, "Shout! For the Lord has given you the city! The city and all that is in it are to be devoted to the Lord. Only Rahab the prostitute and all who are with her in her house shall be spared, because she hid the spies we sent. But keep away from the devoted things, so that you will not bring about your own destruction by taking any of them. Otherwise you will make the camp of Israel liable to destruction and bring trouble on it. All the silver and gold and the articles of bronze and iron are sacred to the Lord and must go into his treasury."

When the trumpets sounded, the people shouted, and at the sound of the trumpet, when the people gave a loud shout, the wall collapsed; so every man charged straight in, and they took the city.

Joshua 6:1–20 (NIV)

How does this equate to a holy sandwich? How is this a working together to extend the kingdom of God? Joshua is operating within the parameters of the kingdom of God. Had he been working within the parameters of the kingdom of self he would have done something very different. We might expect that he would have examined the walled city shut up against his army and gone off straightaway to find other generals who might have had similar experiences in the past and be able to offer him some tactical answers.

As a result of such enquiries he could have planted strings of siege forts around the city and starved them out. He could have cut down trees to make battering rams to break in the gates. He could have used siege catapult engines to lob chunks of rock over the walls with dead animals to poison their water wells. He could have made siege ladders to place against the walls and organise his army to an escalade. And who is to say that such advice from other generals would not have worked just as well?

But no. He did not use his own wisdom or the wisdom of other men as we do when we live and have our being in the kingdom of self. Joshua behaves as though he is living in the kingdom of God and defers to the Almighty for God's wisdom in the matter of pulling down Jericho. It is not for us to determine whose advice might have been more advantageous, it is for us in harmony with God to seek first the kingdom and his righteousness.

And look at God's answer! At first glance it appears to be impossible, incredible, ineffective in the extreme. But Joshua is working together in harmony with God. He does it the way that God wants him to do it. And what way is that? Joshua marches around the outside carrying the message of God and blowing trumpets. Trumpets herald something. They proclaim. Joshua is proclaiming the presence of the living kingdom of God. And because Joshua has done his bit then God acts, he pulls down the walls and lets the army in.

And this is the way that God would see the kingdom

advance into non-Eden situations in churches, families and friends. Joshua did not organise massive prayer groups to persuade God to extend his kingdom. Joshua knew what God wanted to do and how God wanted it done and, in harmony, that's what he did.

CONCLUSION

It is a truth that light can pierce darkness but darkness cannot pierce light. It is only when we recognise that we have wrongly spent too much time standing and working and operating in the kingdom of self, the kingdom of darkness, that we can begin to step towards the light.

It is then that we surrender ourselves to his wisdom in all things. It is a hard step to take. But, having taken it and having found a way to maintain it, to abide in it, then we begin to see the Jerichos of life begin to tumble away.

3

OUR ADOPTION

We are expected to seek a closer walk and work with a Father but too many of us grow up in a world of absent fathers, abusive fathers or fathers who were somewhat less than godly role models. In consequence, attaining a proper, loving and secure relationship with the Almighty Father God can be problematic.

It is in this context that we find it vitally important to understand the nature of new birth and adoption, and the vital importance of being able to share such understandings of God's grace with others.

BEING MADE A NEW CREATION

Being made a new creation is an exciting concept to grow into. This is because who we used to be, before we joined our new family, should have no effect on our new identity after our adoption. In that changeover we inherited a new family history in God's family.

It is the same for all of us. When we become adopted into God's family through the saving work of Christ on the cross, our sins are wiped away by God. One is a new person in Christ, with a clean slate. Our past is rubbed out in him and we change over to being a *new* creation with a *new* name in a new family -- so a new creation but still with the same physical body and still an old nature has to be brought under the control of the Holy Spirit, and there will still be some struggle between new nature and the old 'flesh'!

IS THIS REAL?

In his letter to the Romans, Paul uses the then current Roman view of adoption to describe our new relationship with God, as children of God in this new family.

> For those who are led by the Spirit of God are the children of God. The Spirit you received does not make you slaves, so that you live in fear again; rather, the Spirit you received brought about your adoption to sonship. And by him we cry, "Abba, Father."
>
> The Spirit himself testifies with our spirit that we are God's children. Now if we are children, then we are heirs—heirs of God and co-heirs with Christ, if indeed we share in his sufferings in order that we may also share in his glory.
>
> *Romans 8:14 – 17* (NIV)

The Greek word Paul uses here for 'adoption to sonship' describes the adoption process used time and time again in Roman society in Paul's day. Finding out more about the Roman cultural view of the adoption process can do much to improve our concept of what has happened to us.

> *Patria Potestas* (Roman law) – Encyclopaedia Britannica
> "Patria Potestas, (Latin: "power of a father"), in Roman family law, power that the male head of a family exercised over his children and his more remote descendants in the male line, whatever their age, as well as over those brought into the family by adoption.
>
> This power meant originally not only that he had control over the persons of his children, amounting even to a right to inflict capital punishment, but that he alone had any rights in private law. Thus, possessions of a child became the property of the father. The father might allow a child (as he might a slave) certain property to treat as his own, but in the eye of the law it continued to belong to the father."

OUR ADOPTION

Roman adoption was made a much more serious and a more difficult affair to achieve by the culture of the Roman view of *Patria Potestas*, the father's power over his family, power that was absolute. It was in practice the power of absolute disposal and control, and in the early days of Rome it was also accepted as the power of life and death over, for example, wives involved in adultery.

With regard to his relationship with his father, a Roman son never came of age and, in that sense, never came free from his father's will. No matter his age, he was always under the *Patria Potestas*, in the total possession, and under the total control of, his father.

Obviously, this sense of complete possession and over-riding authority would make adoption into someone else's family a very difficult thing to achieve. It was a serious step to take, and it was never to be taken lightly.

In this Roman adoption process, a person would move from one *Patria Potestas* to another. He was passing out of the possession and control of one father into the equally absolute control and possession of another.

There were two distinct steps to this old Roman process.

Step 1

The first step of the adoption process was called *Mancipatio*, and it was performed through a symbolic act of sale, using copper and scales. This symbolic sale was carried out three times: twice the biological father symbolically sold his son, and twice he bought him back. The third time he sold the son but did not buy him back and in that way his *Patria Potestas* was held to be broken.

This part of the Roman adoption ceremony was carried out in the presence of seven witnesses. Their presence did two things: it supported the new father's application to the magistrates in the second adoption step, and provided a safeguard for the future.

To understand this safeguard we might imagine a

hypothetical situation where an adopting father had died, and there followed some dispute or other about the right of the adopted son to inherit. In such a case, one or more of the original seven witnesses could step forward and swear that the adoption was indeed genuine and true. Thus the right of the adopted person is guaranteed by the witnesses and he enters into his inheritance.

Step 2

When the sale was over, there followed a second ceremony called *vindicatio*, from which we derive the word 'vindication'. The new adopting father went to a Praetor, a Roman magistrate, and presented him with a legal and witnessed case for the transference of the person to be adopted into his own *Patria Potestas*.

When both these stages were properly fulfilled, the adoption was complete. Clearly this was a serious and very impressive step to take. But it is the consequences of Roman adoption which are most significant for us in the picture that is in Paul's mind when he refers to us as being adopted.

There were four main consequences to this adoption process:

• The adopted person lost all rights to his old family, and gained all the rights of a fully legitimate son in his new family. In the most literal sense, and in the most legally binding way, he got a new father.
• Because of this he became an heir to his new father's estate. Even if other sons were born after the event, although such offspring would have been seen as real blood relations, their arrival in the family would not affect his rights. He was solidly and securely a co-heir with them.
• In the eyes of the law, the old life of the adopted person was completely wiped out. For example, all debts were legally cancelled; they were wiped out as though they had never been. The adopted person was thought of as being a

new person entering into a new life with which the past had no connection.
• In the eyes of the law, the adopted person was literally and absolutely the son of the new father.

It is through Paul's analogy that he explains our own adoption process – that when someone becomes a Christian they are switched over to join the actual family of God. Such people do nothing to deserve it; God the great Father, in his amazing love and mercy, takes the lost, helpless, spiritually poverty-stricken, debt-laden sinner and adopts him into his own family, so that the debts are cancelled and the glory inherited.

So, in the final and most significant part of the process of Roman adoption, in the eyes of the law, the adopted child became seen and accepted as an absolute child of the new father.

HISTORICAL EVIDENCE

History has left us with an excellent example of how completely this new relationship was taken on board in those days: the Emperor Claudius adopted Nero, in order that Nero would succeed him on the throne. These two men were not related in any way at all. They were not blood relatives. We know that in fact Claudius already had a child, his daughter, Octavia.

Nero set out to marry Octavia to cement his new inheritance alliance with the family. Now, Nero and Octavia were not in any way true blood relatives; but, in the eyes of the law, they were brother and sister. So before they could get married, the Roman Senate had to vote on and pass special legislation to enable Nero to marry someone who was, legally, his own sister.

SOME OTHER TRUTH APPLICATIONS
• "For those who are led by the Spirit of God are the children of God."

Or, put another way in Roman terms, we are in God's *Patria Potestas*. We are the property of God, owned and possessed by him.

• "The Spirit you received does not make you slaves, so that you live in fear again; rather, the Spirit you received brought about your adoption to sonship. And by him we cry, "Abba, Father." This is an expression of sureness, a certainty of awareness of our sonship!

• "The Spirit himself testifies with our spirit that we are God's children." Here is the eternal Holy Spirit who witnesses to our adoption as sons. God's Spirit witnesses with our spirit that we really are God's children.

Paul tells us that it is the Holy Spirit himself who is the witness to our adoption into the family of God. We do not need seven witnesses when we have a witness who is eternal and is God.

• "Now if we are children, then we are heirs—heirs of God and co-heirs with Christ, if indeed we share in his sufferings in order that we may also share in his glory."

We are joint heirs with Christ, equal in inheritance. Christ is also the firstborn among MANY brothers!

THE ANALOGY
We cannot stretch our Roman cultural illustration any further beyond its biblical intent. Every aspect of an illustrative analogy will eventually break down just because it is only a temporal picture of an eternal truth.

But we have discovered from this a new and a rich historical and cultural background to the facts of Roman adoption. It does help us gain greater insight to the mind of Paul the Apostle when he speaks of our adoption as children of God in the Roman cultural context of the day.

OUR ADOPTION

PLANNING WITH HIM, ACTING WITH HIM

Clearly, this adoption process has not happened just so that we can go about our daily business as we did before and have some powerful help from on high when we need it! In the Roman adoption process that we see in Paul's picture, we become subservient to the Father. The Father does not become subservient to the child!

Of course he would wish to help us in our times of need:

> [Jesus said] "If you, then, though you are evil, know how to give good gifts to your children, how much more will your Father in heaven give good gifts to those who ask him!
>
> *Matthew 7:11*

But this cannot be the main thrust of our relationship with our adoptive Father.

Paul's view of this, through his knowledge of Roman culture, is that it is the Father (not us) who is the driver in the relationship. It is the Father who has the power of absolute disposal and control. The obedient child then should be constantly seeking the will of the Father rather than only speaking to him when his help is needed.

QUOTATION

> "It is clear that he does not pray, who, far from uplifting himself to God, requires that God shall lower Himself to him, and who resorts to prayer not to stir the man in us to will what God wills, but only to persuade God to will what the man in us wills."
>
> *Thomas Aquinas* (1225–1274)

WORKING AND WALKING CLOSER
Our main drive in relationship with God in prayer must be to "stir the man in us to will what God wills". To major on what *he* wants, rather than majoring on what *we* want, brings us closer to him and to the world in the mind of Christ. Being closer means working much more in harmony with him. Being more in harmony with him means being far more effective, and that by *his* measurement of such things and not by ours.

GOING WITH IT
Accepting Paul's view of adoption, stepping over from one family to another means stepping over from one *kingdom* into another. We step from the kingdom of the world into the kingdom of God. We know that:
• The kingdom of the world is where we allow our lives to be run by the great god 'ME' or 'I'. It is the 'self kingdom'.
• The systems we use to run the world, politics, economics and others, these are centred on self: wealth, self-promotion, self-comfort. Our inter-relationship with others is often self-centred, criticism, manipulation etc.
• Such 'self-centred thoughts and deeds are in the kingdom of self, the kingdom of the world, the kingdom of darkness, subject to the sinful nature.
• These things are not God-centred, not kingdom-centred, not seeking to be in the new Father's will, not seeking the kingdom of God and his righteousness.

USEFUL HINTS
To test oneself, to see if we really have understood the results of adoption and obedience, we would do well to listen to how we pray, and how we ourselves think and speak about our Christian life on our own or with others, our Christian and church experiences. We would do well to check the number of times we use the words 'ME' or 'I' when we speak of such things.

THE LORD'S PRAYER
"Your kingdom come, your will be done, on earth as it is in heaven...."

We can use this prayer to mean:

"We'd like the world to be a nice place rather than the nasty place it is."

"We'd like the nasty people straightened out to be more like us."

"Your will is bound to be something good otherwise you wouldn't will it. We need more of something good."

"I've no idea what your will actually is but I can only hope that it's what I want. And will do me some good"

But in seeking to work in harmony with our heavenly Father we actually want to fall into a life of being obedient to the Father, to be at peace, to be in total harmony with him. Such vague understandings of his will do not allow for obedience.

> "You will have these tassels to look at and so you will remember all the commands of the Lord, that you may obey them and not prostitute yourselves by chasing after the lusts of your own hearts and eyes. Then you will remember to obey all my commands and will be consecrated to your God. I am the Lord your God, who brought you out of Egypt to be your God. I am the Lord your God.'"
>
> *Numbers 15:39–41* (NIV)

and:

> So I find this law at work: Although I want to do good, evil is right there with me. For in my inner being I delight in God's law; but I see another law at work in me, waging war against the law of my mind and making me a prisoner of the law of sin at work within me.
>
> What a wretched man I am! Who will rescue me from

this body that is subject to death? Thanks be to God, who delivers me through Jesus Christ our Lord!"
Romans 7: 21 – 25 (NIV)

Let us continue with Paul's striving, and in humility like his, put behind us the self-life of the sinful nature and attain the life that Christ wants for us! We need the constant help and in-filling of the Holy Spirit in this walk of sanctification.

GROWING TOGETHER

Working harmony in the Roman home vitally depended on the children's obedience, on their living in their father's will. Memories will always have been with them, but adopted children would set out to put their old lives utterly behind them and have their being as part of their new father's household.

To translate that culture into today as an encouragement to greater involvement in church life would be to vastly undervalue the intent. The key is to seek first the kingdom of God, to resist the easy temptations of the self-life, the "I" life, the "I" kingdom, ways of looking at life that are "I" centred.

We must first seek his kingdom and to live in his righteousness and then the promised blessings may follow.

AN OVERALL VIEW

Jesus Christ is the Lord of lords, the King of all kings. We might say that our God is the Majesty above all Majesties, the President above all Presidents. He owns the whole world. We did not choose him in order to get ourselves adopted by this majestically powerful King. He has chosen to adopt us.

As with the symbolism of the Roman process of adoption so we have come under the *Patria Potestas* of our heavenly Father. We were bought at a price. Jesus, the divine Son, gave himself as a sacrifice, dying in our place, taking the punishment that our sins deserved.

OUR ADOPTION

God, in his grace and mercy, chose to take us into his own household under his rule of *Patria Potestas*. We are not given the liberty of coming of age and leaving home to do our own thing. To do that would mean falling back into being away from home and reverting to use our own 'wisdom' again – the mark of being in the wrong kingdom, of having the wrong 'god'.

Theologically, a person may feel they have the right 'god'. Christian upbringing and experience might lead us to think that we have the right 'god', but if we are using our *own* wisdom instead of the Father's then we may still be operating in the wrong kingdom, the kingdom whose 'god' is self.

So it is well worth keeping a constant check on ourselves. If we say we have no sin we deceive ourselves and the truth is not in us. But our sin may not only be actual acts and thoughts that rise up in us from time to time, they may be merely an ongoing existence in a kingdom driven by the wrong 'god'. That would be sin indeed!

Abiding in God's kingdom, his household, means that all that we have belongs to him. Our homes actually do not belong to us, they belong to him. Under his *Patria Potestas* such money that might come our way is all his, he merely makes us an allowance in order to maintain what is his, take care of what is his, and bless his other children through us. We owe him everything.

Much of the peace and the joy and blessing of living in this working harmony with him in his family comes from our 'having the mind of Christ' or knowing his revealed will. Knowing this will not automatically of course make us any 'better' at being Christians! What it will do is produce humility. Humility is the bloom and the blossom of holiness, and without holiness no one will see the Lord. If ever we see supposed 'holiness' without humility we know that it is a counterfeit.

The majestic Heavenly Father is the one who requires us to work with him in his business of kingdom growing. It is he who requires it to be so. What a privilege to be allowed to work in his kingdom under him!

4

A MORE WORTHY PRIESTHOOD

AN OPEN HEAVEN?
It is sometimes announced excitedly, "Our church is under an open heaven!" By this proclamation the church concerned desires to tell the world that some restoration miracle(s) have taken place within its walls. And those acts of God have been witnessed and accepted by its leaders and/or its members.

It might be easy, in our cynicism, to write off such statements as mere forms of advertising, whilst at the same time we hold a secret longing for such things to happen as a result of our own prayers! We would quietly love to see heaven open above us and our church, so that God can deal with the dreadful things of life easily through our ministrations, and so that we and others can be quickly and easily healed.

COULD WE LIVE UNDER AN OPEN HEAVEN?
We must beware, in today's church environment, of suggesting that heaven opens above certain people, or certain places, implying that God is especially favouring individuals. his will in such things can easily be misconstrued.

It is the cross that has opened heaven, and Christ died for the sins of the whole world. 'Opening heaven' is not something he does sovereignly and without the co-operation of the saints. It does not happen only because we pray hard for it to be so. There are things we need to do in response to the saving death and resurrection of Jesus. We need to deepen our relationship with him, being always ready to follow the prompting of the Spirit to follow where he leads and do what he is giving us to do.

DEEPER AND DEEPER

The proper basis for an apparently 'open heaven' is this: the deeper the relationship between Christ and us, the greater the harmony and the easier the flow of the benefits of heavenly grace into the world.

So this is a relational issue, not one of theology or spirituality or style or technique in ministry. It is a tightening of our relationship with the living, active God.

What we need is to be flowing more readily in the flow of grace. The appearance of an 'open heaven' is undeniably a sovereign work of God. But the believers are involved. Often in such situations people have been praying, sometimes for years. There needs to be a real and seeking for hunger for the Lord and his righteousness. He sees that heartfelt desire for him.

GOD MAKES HIS MOVE

God has already moved in this relational issue by descending in Jesus, below the angels, to get down to our human size, as it were, to help us. Jesus died for the sins of the whole world so his commitment to mankind has already been demonstrated. It is total. His offer to us that we can be workers in his kingdom is complete and full.

Always completely God and always a completely sinless human, Jesus' movement towards us is full – all it ever will be. The response to this God-movement, to complete the divine design, is that our discipleship should result in our moving from just being totally human to being Jesus-like as well.

To cement any working kingdom relationship between us

and God we must accept that he has already made his move towards us, and now we need to move more towards him. We do this by allowing to grow within us the mind of Christ. The more this happens, the more we humans can think like him and the more the Spirit moves us within his will. Thus it is that we become naturally more obedient, more in harmony with him and his will.

> "What we have received is not the spirit of the world, but the Spirit who is from God, so that we may understand what God has freely given us.
>
> This is what we speak, not in words taught us by human wisdom but in words taught by the Spirit, explaining spiritual realities with Spirit-taught words.
>
> The person without the Spirit does not accept the things that come from the Spirit of God but considers them foolishness, and cannot understand them because they are discerned only through the Spirit.
>
> The person with the Spirit makes judgments about all things, but such a person is not subject to merely human judgments, for, "Who has known the mind of the Lord so as to instruct him?" But we have the mind of Christ."
>
> *1 Corinthians 2:12–16* (NIV)

REMEMBER ADOPTION?

Earlier, we discussed Paul's understanding of the culture of Roman adoption. Here, after adoption, the adopted child never came of age as we might understand that today.

Our Western culture now allows for us, after a given birthday has been reached, to leave home. We are still related to our parents but are no longer subject to them. We do not have to obey their decisions. Rather, we are expected to use commonsense and worldly wisdom to make our own way in the world. We don't have to remain in harmony with them any more.

In the Roman culture of adoption that Paul understood, when describing our new relationship with our heavenly Father, that time of 'coming of age' never occurred.

It was culturally deeply held that an adopted child, in exactly the same way that would occur with a natural born child, would always be obedient to and owned by his father. He or she might physically move away from home and live elsewhere with his own new earthly family, but that seeking of his father's will – and the peace and security of dwelling within it – was always present.

Our ongoing obedience is absolutely essential to life, and to our life in Christ, today. The more we journey towards becoming like him, as someone developing the mind of Christ, the more we can move like him – and stay that way.

> "Remain in me, as I also remain in you. No branch can bear fruit by itself; it must remain in the vine. Neither can you bear fruit unless you remain in me.
>
> "I am the vine; you are the branches. If you remain in me and I in you, you will bear much fruit; apart from me you can do nothing.
>
> If you do not remain in me, you are like a branch that is thrown away and withers; such branches are picked up, thrown into the fire and burned."
>
> *John 15:4–6* (NIV)

And, as our minds are renewed, so we will find that working within his will and obeying it becomes a far more natural and joyful process.

> "Therefore, I urge you, brothers and sisters, in view of God's mercy, to offer your bodies as a living sacrifice, holy and pleasing to God—this is your true and proper worship. Do not conform to the pattern of this world, but be transformed by the renewing of your mind. Then you

will be able to test and approve what God's will is—his good, pleasing and perfect will."

Romans 12:1–2 (NIV)

Heaven's opening is the drawing back of an already torn veil between heaven and earth that enables us to suddenly see into heaven more clearly.

"In my thirtieth year, in the fourth month on the fifth day, while I was among the exiles by the Kebar River, the heavens were opened and I saw visions of God."

[Ezekiel's Inaugural Vision] *Ezekiel 1:1* (NIV)

SOMETHING THAT HAPPENED TO JESUS

At that time Jesus came from Nazareth in Galilee and was baptized by John in the Jordan. Just as Jesus was coming up out of the water, he saw heaven being torn open and the Spirit descending on him like a dove. And a voice came from heaven: "You are my Son, whom I love; with you I am well pleased."

Mark 1:9–11 (NIV)

And it was apparent at the stoning of Stephen

When the members of the Sanhedrin heard this, they were furious and gnashed their teeth at him. But Stephen, full of the Holy Spirit, looked up to heaven and saw the glory of God, and Jesus standing at the right hand of God. "Look," he said, "I see heaven open and the Son of Man standing at the right hand of God."

Acts 7:54–56 (NIV)

Elijah saw the heavens opened on Mt Carmel, and three apostles saw it happen at the transfiguration. Elisha is used in healing miracles whereas servant Gehazi seems to fail while using exactly the same technique.

Interestingly, episodes recorded in the Bible of heaven opening seem to occur so that the watcher can see into heaven. He looks up and looks in. When today we claim that our church or our organization is 'under an open heaven' we usually mean something quite opposite – that heaven is pouring down onto earth. That pouring, because of the work of the Cross, is actually happening all over the world to – and onto – every church, and everywhere Christians live and gather together.

As, unhappily, most of us have our being in the self-kingdom we cannot recognize this fact of grace.

WHO THEN CAN SEE THIS HAPPEN?

Answer? A holy priesthood, and the church of believers is described as a royal priesthood (whose great High Priest is Jesus, its head) and it should include many who have set out to surrender themselves to the idea of returning willingly into the original relationship that Adam had with God in Eden.

Adam and Eve were created in God's image. They were able to live comfortably in the kingdom, in total confidence in God's will and obedience to it. They lived in it and walked in it and all the blessings followed that spiritual life of living in his will. Losing the abundant life in his will was the greatest hidden cost of the Fall.

But, before that disaster, they not only lived under an open heaven, they lived in it! They could have been described, before the Fall, as being a worthy priesthood. God's will was actively and easily achieved through them and through their lives.

HOW DO WE BECOME THAT WORTHY?

The answer lies in these hinge pin verses from the Sermon on the Mount. In speaking these words Jesus is showing us a road back to becoming a holy priesthood under him, people through whom God's kingdom can be fulfilled because of a tighter working relationship.

> "But seek first his kingdom and his righteousness, and all these things will be given to you as well."
>
> *Matthew 6:33* (NIV)

Seek first his kingdom and his righteousness? Many interpret this sentence as meaning simply "try and be more like Jesus" without discussing the practicalities of seeking. Others water this passage down in their teaching by simply quoting it as telling us to seek God whenever we need him.

But to seek to go back to living in his kingdom implies that we currently live in another one somewhere, otherwise we would already be within that life that Jesus calls us to seek.

To seek his righteousness implies that we are somewhat short of all his virtues, something less than godly, something less than the image of God in which he wanted to have us live in this world.

So the Christian pilgrim must press on! We must hold in view that there are two kingdoms in this world: the kingdom of God and the one so many of us live in, the kingdom of self. How do they differ? How do we travel from one, across its frontiers, to the other one? How do we lack his righteousness, and how do we become more like him and live in his kingdom?

If we can do this, just as Adam and Eve once did in the Garden of Eden, the blessings will naturally follow the righteous kingdom life. Adam and Eve in their unfallen state did not need ministries of preaching, healing, evangelism, mission, etc. They walked in everlasting life and had no sickness. The kingdom blessings filled their lives just because of the way they lived, and who they lived with – God.

To stare at our own lives is not the way forward into the kingdom of God. If we live in the light there might be enough light to show us bits of darkness within us but if we live in the darkness there will not be enough light to show us the shadows.

So, as we shall learn, it is better to admit to God that we do not know the way to become more holy. We can only beg for his Spirit to work within us and that we might make plenty of room for him through his work of sanctifying us. In this way we will hope to lose some of our own worldly wisdom and make more space for the mind of Christ.

Growing in awareness of the mind of Christ, we become more in harmony with the Father. The relationship tightens. And in and through that harmony alone can be seen a greater harvest of kingdom fruit.

5

HIS KINGDOM, OUR KINGDOM

So God created mankind in his own image, in the image of God he created them; male and female he created them

Genesis 1:27 (NIV)

EDEN DREAMING
[This is Mike Endicott reflecting, meditating]

One evening, in the dusky twilight, God came walking through Eden, looking forward to his usual time of talking with his friend, Adam. He was coming to keep their regular rendezvous, in the usual place at the normal time.

No doubt he was looking forward to it, a flavour of anticipation in his mouth.

But was God about to be disappointed? It may seem as though the first one to be disappointed on this earth was not one of us human beings at all, but God himself!

Surely, Adam usually came here expectantly, perhaps elated, with a happy, smiling face, with his hands outstretched in welcome. But, this time, Adam did not arrive. He let God down; he failed to arrive at the agreed time of meeting.

So God went to look for him. Not satisfied just to arrive and then leave the meeting place in the trees, he set out to find his friend. God is not satisfied merely with the rituals of arrangements, with meetings, with keeping appointments, with following agendas – he wants our company. He hungered for his friend and for the friendship of the man on whom he had placed the imprint of his own image. They had, after all, a great deal in common.

WHO WAS THIS ADAM?

Adam and Eve were created directly by God, to live in Eden, in his kingdom. Here they lived abundant lives that had three main attributes we should take note of:

• They were created in God's image. He had imprinted himself on them. They thought much like he did, in harmony with him. They were, as it were, Christ-like.

• They had authority over everything. They were entrusted with ruling the world on God's behalf. The trust God placed in them to do this stems from the nature of their tight relationship with him.

• The blessings were not sought, they followed them along through life. They lived in complete peace and good health. They lived holy lives in the kingdom of God.

There lay over them only one rule, one kingdom, Eden, the kingdom of God.

THE FALL

"Now the serpent was more crafty than any of the wild animals the Lord God had made. He said to the woman, "Did God really say, 'You must not eat from any tree in the garden'?"

The woman said to the serpent, "We may eat fruit from the trees in the garden, but God did say, 'You must not eat fruit from the tree that is in the middle of the garden, and you must not touch it, or you will die.'"

"You will not certainly die," the serpent said to the woman. "For God knows that when you eat from it your eyes will be opened, and you will be like God, knowing good and evil."

When the woman saw that the fruit of the tree was good

for food and pleasing to the eye, and also desirable for gaining wisdom, she took some and ate it. She also gave some to her husband, who was with her, and he ate it."

Genesis 3:1–7 (NIV)

Adam and Eve were attracted by the idea of having their own wisdom. With worldly wisdom they would no longer have to refer to God. They could make decisions to suit themselves first.

So, in surrendering to that temptation and eating the fruit against God's express will, they brought into reality another kingdom, the kingdom of self! Here it would be that they themselves would rule. Here they could make their own decisions with their own wisdom as they had wanted to, when they met the serpent in Eden.

This new kingdom is referred to in this book as the 'self' kingdom or the 'self' world as it is ruled by the god called 'self'. This self-kingdom is run on the fuel of human wisdom.

In it the blessings of the Eden life do not follow the lifestyle. Sin and sickness and death have come into the world. Some medical professionals today claim that at least 90% of all sickness is the result of stress – and stress is the outworking of pressures that roam around in the self-life

As there are today still two kingdoms so there are two distinct sorts of wisdom – *God's* wisdom and our *own* ideas. Scripture calls us to use God's wisdom by seeking his righteousness, living in his kingdom and knowing the mind of Christ.

TWO KINDS OF WISDOM

Who is wise and understanding among you? Let them show it by his good life, by deeds done in the humility that comes from wisdom. But if you harbour bitter envy and selfish ambition in your hearts, do not boast about it or deny the truth. Such "wisdom" does not come down from heaven but is earthly, unspiritual, of the devil. For where you have envy and selfish ambition, there you find disorder and every evil practice.

But the wisdom that comes from heaven is first of all pure; then peace-loving, considerate, submissive, full of mercy and good fruit, impartial and sincere.

Peacemakers who sow in peace reap a harvest of righteousness.

James 3:13–18 (NIV)

THE EFFECTS OF THE FALL
[This is Mike Endicott reflecting, meditating]

Meanwhile, back in Eden...

Wanting the pleasure of some conversation, God started off at once around the garden to find the man. The voice that spoke a universe into being now echoed through the Eden woods, the same voice that could bring life and such beauty to the planet, that could bring enormous adoration and reverence from countless angels.

"Where are you?"

All God's heart, all his power, is in this soft voice, talking to one man, to you, to me. The breeze in the garden has died away so that we can hear this voice with its new gentle whisper. The birds have quietened their song to allow for this new Eden music in a mellow minor key. Creation in the vicinity of the garden is holding its breath. God is holding his heart still, to catch our first response to his call.

"Where are you?"

OUR LOSSES

In the Fall, in giving in to the temptation to rule the world ourselves with our own wisdom, we gave up a great proportion of Adam and Eve's three main attributes:

• They were created in God's image. Still largely relying on our own wisdom, we have consequently lost a great deal of the 'mind of Christ'. So how could our working relationship with him ever be a tight one?

• They had authority over everything. We have given up authority over all the world's managing systems that so need God's wisdom to manage them.

• The blessings were not sought, they followed. Now we travel most of the time in the self kingdom and turn, often only when in trouble, to seek blessings. Even work, by and large, is not a joy any more but a curse. We are caught up in the 'self' kingdom's cycle of working, consuming, working, consuming.

Kingdom Discipleship is vital. We disciples can easily be present in one kingdom whilst living in another (the 'self' world and God's kingdom).

> "Consider how the wild flowers grow. They do not labour or spin. Yet I tell you, not even Solomon in all his splendour was dressed like one of these. If that is how God clothes the grass of the field, which is here today, and tomorrow is thrown into the fire, how much more will he clothe you—you of little faith! And do not set your heart on what you will eat or drink; do not worry about it. For the pagan world runs after all such things, and your Father knows that you need them. But seek his kingdom, and these things will be given to you as well.
>
> "Do not be afraid, little flock, for your Father has been pleased to give you the kingdom."
>
> *Luke 12:27–32* (NIV)

PRAYER IN THE CONTEXT OF THE 'ABIDING' REQUIRED

> "But seek first his kingdom and his righteousness, and all these things will be given to you as well."
>
> *Matthew 6:33* (NIV)

This is a call to return to the kingdom life, the Eden life where the blessings follow the life. It is not only a call to seek God, or even to seek his kingdom. It is most importantly a call to seek a life lived in his righteousness.

We are not called to live in the 'self' world and flit back over the border every time we need God to do something for us. We are called to 'abide', back in his kingdom.

LIVING IN THE 'SELF' WORLD

This is a way of living that is centred on our own means and ends. Easily seen in the great systems of politics and economics, it is full of self-power, self-love, self-promotion, self-confidence, self-comfort. Our major decisions are made to improve the lot of self.

Rather than living in God's kingdom, we too might be accused of living in this world whilst at the same time worshipping God and requiring much of him so that we can continue living as easily as possible with the consequences of the 'self' world.

With no comprehension of there being these two kingdoms, we live on in the 'self' place until something goes wrong. Then we pray to invoke God's will concerning our problems and the effects of those problems. Then, if we are blessed by grace, we can travel on as before.

> When you ask, you do not receive, because you ask with wrong motives, that you may spend what you get on your pleasures.
>
> *James 4:3* (NIV)

To seek his righteousness is the way back from the 'self' kingdom to the kingdom of God where the blessings flow and follow.

"I am the vine; you are the branches. If you remain in me and I in you, you will bear much fruit; apart from me you can do nothing." *John 15:5* (NIV)

SPECIFIC REPENTANCE NEEDED?
How easy it is to repent of minor things, to invoke God's forgiveness – and go on as before! How easy it is to repent of the act of stealing a pencil from the workplace without realising a far greater sin; that the paper clip episode was only a symptom of a great mistake. That comparatively minor act should have shown us that we are still living in the 'self' kingdom, the kingdom centred on self. And self is the wrong God.

Lord, have mercy, and help us to walk on into the kingdom of light.

6

TRUSTING THE LORD

IS THIS ONLY ONE WAY TRUST?
Adam and Eve were entrusted with ruling the world on God's behalf. This trust that God placed in them to do this ruling stems from the nature of their single-minded relationship with him. He trusted Adam and Eve because they lived in God's likeness; we might say today that they had the mind of Christ, so they could be utterly trusted to say and do the right thing.

FAITH AND TRUST
But what about us, and our trusting him? To be used effectively by Almighty God we have to trust him too.

May we ask a certain question in our kingdom humility: we know that he can change things but, if we are specific in our request, should we expect our prayers to be answered in the way we want, or do we think this might be trying to manipulate God?

Could it be that God hears our prayers and *then* makes up his mind how to answer them? Could it be that we do not therefore know his will when we pray? If we do not know what he wants to do, are we trusting him to do whatever he thinks is best? We may like to think that we trust him but if we do not see answers then how do we trust?

But if our awareness of relationship with God really is secure we would be moving with him in his will when we pray for people, or with people. Such harmony sees heaven's grace infiltrating the problem to hand.

ANALOGY – THE WHEELBARROW OF TRUST
"I will trust and not be afraid" *Isaiah 12:2* (NIV)

Most of us would struggle to be anxious for nothing at all, but we can learn to rely on God if we know the difference between faith and trust. Let's imagine you're near the beautiful but dangerous Niagara Falls. A circus performer has strung a rope across the falls with the intention of pushing a wheelbarrow from one side to the other. Just before stepping on the rope, he asks you,

"Do you think I can accomplish this feat?"

His reputation has preceded him, so you reply that you believe he can walk the tightrope. In other words, you have faith that he will succeed. Then he says, "If you really believe I can do it, how about getting in the wheelbarrow and crossing with me?" Accepting his invitation would be an example of remarkable trust.

It isn't difficult for some people to believe that God is capable of performing mighty deeds. After all, he created the entire universe. Trust, however, requires that we depend on him to keep his promises to us even when there is no proof that he will. It's not so easy to get into that wheelbarrow and put our lives in his care. Yet it's a step we must take if we are to be anxious for nothing in all of life's circumstances.

TWO-WAY DEAL
If the reader is in a business partnership with someone, working together for a common end, sharing skills and energies to achieve a common goal, then the whole thing has to be based in this very particularly sought after kind of relating called 'trust'. The partners have to trust each other at a very deep basic level. There are of course many other aspects to a business partnership, skills, shared visions, shared values etc. All such things will in due course be

exercised, but all must be served up on the underlying support of trust.

It's the same with any personal relationship partnership. Marriage partners may do a thousand different things together, but the relationship will only last at any depth where there is an underlying, unspoken layer of trust running right through everything.

And the same idea follows with our working relationship with God. It must be built on an underlying layer of trust. The lack of this trust underlay is one major cause for the dearth of miracles seen in the bow-wave of the kingdom today as it stretches forwards in the world.

NAZARETH

There is a cancerous sickness in the church these days which we will refer to as the 'Nazareth syndrome'. It was there in Nazareth that things went wrong. It was only there that Jesus could do very few restoring miracles. Why? The inhabitants had got him out of focus.

Jesus had gone there and preached and his listeners accepted him for what he was, but only partially. They knew him to be Mary's son and a carpenter, and that his own family were in the congregation, but they missed his role as Son of God. They got him out of focus.

This misapprehension is the most serious of evils and this out of focus image of Jesus stalks our pews and pulpits to this very day. Why serious? Because it's exactly the same trick that the serpent played on Eve in the Garden of Eden.

They had been clearly told not to eat the fruit from a particular tree as it would cause them to die. The serpent managed to persuade Eve that God was just a spoilsport, a party-pooper – and that his words were of little serious consequence.

So she got God out of focus and we have to live with the shocking consequences to this hour. And all because she allowed Satan to de-focus her image of God and she was led into disobedience. That episode was the leverage behind the Fall. And most of us have allowed precisely the same thing to occur in our own spiritual lives, without realising it.

If we want to see harmony in our working relationship with God in this way we will need to work and pray, every day, to bring the real Jesus of the Gospels more and more into focus in our own thoughts, so that we can see more clearly the kingdom of God.

It's going to be problematic to live in the kingdom, proclaim it and see the consequent dynamics of the kingdom at work, without seeing both it and the character of its King as clearly as we can. It is simply not possible, despite all our protestation to the contrary, to trust someone when we are not confident concerning what they might do. Of course we are often wonderfully surprised by God and nothing I am saying here should be be taken as denying or detracting from that. If we read the Acts of the Apostles we see that the believers constantly saw God doing new things. God is sovereign and free. What I mean is that we should begin to expect him to do what he has said he will do and to act in line with his promises and his will that he has already revealed in his Word.

The eye is the lamp of the body. When our eyes are focusing rightly, our whole body is in the light. But if our eyes are badly focused, our whole body will be full of darkness. If we have a misty, obscure idea of who God is, and if our ideas don't accord with his self-revelation, then we need to go back to the scriptures and get our 'picture' of who he is, and his character, in line with the truth.

THE SOURCE OF TROUBLE IS OUR WISDOM

Adam and Eve saw that the forbidden fruit was good for food, tasty, and good for getting wisdom. Armed then with their own wisdom they fell backwards into the world of self, the self-kingdom where self rules. And the first thing many of us do with that human wisdom is to built a picture of God out of our experiences of him, and not out of the scriptural descriptions of him. That is using our own wisdom to define God. We finish up with a 'god' we think may well be able to help his people but, frankly, that's unlikely.

Not only is Jesus the centre of the kingdom, he is the kingdom. It follows that, should we have an albeit slightly out-of-focus conception of his character and his will, then we might be conversing with an out-of-focus idea of God. Even with the best intentions, we may miss the target with an unfocused eye. It might all look right to us, but we might be yoked to the wrong horse!

Out of focus, those ways of God's working with and through us that require us to trust him are consequently and dramatically reduced. Thus it is that the Christian church's evangelism and our witness to the world is often hard work and often, sadly, of little real consequence. The early Christian kingdom inhabitants appear to have found their work of evangelism and healing the sick and injured to be a far more joyful and fruitful experience than we do!

ME?

So we should be prepared, in an honest and childlike way, to have our image of Christ continuously challenged by the portrayal of his character in scripture. What do others say about this?

> I would very earnestly ask you to check your conception of Christ, the image of him which, as a Christian, you hold in your mind, with the actual revealed Person who can be seen and studied in action in the pages of the Gospels.
>
> We may think that it is of some value to hold in our minds a bundle of assorted ideals to influence and control our conduct. But surely we need to be very careful before we give that "bundle" the name of Jesus Christ the Son of God.
>
> *J. B. Phillips* (1906–1982)

Not only do we not know God except through Jesus Christ; we do not even know ourselves except through Jesus Christ.

Blaise Pascal (1623–1662), *Pensees* (Thoughts)[1660], P. F. Collier & Son, 1910, #548, p. 177

HOW COULD THIS BE?
How could our understanding of God possibly get out of focus in the first place? How could we possibly become yoked up to the wrong horse? Well, Christians living in the self kingdom allow their experience of life to get in the way, and that experience attacks childlike trust.

"Once I was asked," reports one Christian, "to pray for five little boys, all aged about six years old, who had cancer of the blood. Four died soon afterwards and the fifth went into remission for a year and then himself went on to glory."

To a greater or lesser extent, this sort of thing is a heartbreaking experience commonly encountered by many a praying Christian.

"As they died, I received five large though subconscious blows to my trust in God to restore life," he continues. "I turned to the church and listened eagerly to what seemed like good reasons for God's mysterious and apparent failure to save these children."

Much second-guessing about God's intentions has been drip fed to us over many years, but the end result is always the same -- our image of Jesus is tarnished, knocked off track, pushed out of focus. He has in our estimate become a little less reliable and, therefore, a little less trustworthy. We cannot help this slippage in our thinking -- we are human beings, after all.

We begin to be assured more and more from our experience that persuading God to restore anything is not easy, and such a compassionate God rarely responds in the way we think he surely should. We build our own personal theologies accordingly.

"But now I know in my heart," says the Christian with new appreciation, "that the real Christ, the Jesus shown in the pages of the Gospels, rather than the one whose character I had built out of my own experiences, never failed to bring quick and complete restoration to all who came and asked him, with as little as a mustard seed of expectancy that he would do it."

TWO KINGDOMS AGAIN

The kingdom of God is ruled by our God who never never refused to heal anyone, never decided to give a sufferer something else other than that which they had asked for. And Jesus Christ was, and is, the perfect image of the invisible God.

On the other hand the self kingdom in which we live relies on our own wisdom to build the image of God that we feel is right and reasonable from our Christian experience. So those living in that kingdom pray to a different 'god' other than the one portrayed by Jesus. The wrong picture is of an unreliable and vague deity, probably not very active.

PAUL'S UNDERSTANDING

> I hope you will put up with a little of my foolishness; but you are already doing that. I am jealous for you with a godly jealousy. I promised you to one husband, to Christ, so that I might present you as a pure virgin to him. But I am afraid that just as Eve was deceived by the serpent's cunning, your minds may somehow be led astray from your sincere and pure devotion to Christ.
>
> For if someone comes to you and preaches a Jesus other than the Jesus we preached, or if you receive a different spirit from the one you received, or a different gospel from

the one you accepted, you put up with it easily enough."
2 Corinthians 11:1–4 (NIV)

DISCERNING THE DIFFERENCE

So how can we discern between these two, the true risen Christ as revealed to us in the New Testament and the one somehow reshaped out of focus from our often not-so-happy prayer experiences as Christians?

There are three easy ways to tell the difference –

• The out-of-focus 'Jesus' pictured in the kingdom of self can often be something of a mystery when it comes to helping us out with practical problems like family difficulties and sickness. We can never really be sure of his reaction to prayer but we pray to him anyway in the hope that he might intervene in some good and constructive way. We realise that effective prayer means praying into his will for the given circumstances and, because we have little idea of that will, gifts of discernment are much sought after to ease the prayer journey.

In complete contrast to this picture of God today, the real in-focus Jesus Christ (the one on whose character is modelled the kingdom of God) never hesitated to heal someone who needed it and who asked for it with a mustard seed of expectancy that he would actually do it.

He taught us that God is a Father who is willing to supply our needs just as he supplies the needs of the birds of the air and the flowers of the field.

• The out-of-focus God will often be credited with having a deep, mysterious and yet somehow benevolent reason for not offering healing to someone who is sick or injured.

In contrast, every single person who came to the gospel Jesus for healing was healed. The real Jesus never suggested or behaved in any way as if there might be a deep purpose for anyone remaining ill. He never hesitated for one moment. He never had to pray to determine whether he should heal because he knew that the permanent and constant will of the Father is to do it.

• The common and often out-of-focus vision of God that stalks our pews and pulpits is said to be in complete control; his power is thought of as being absolute and yet somehow he completely fails to show this power reliably and consistently to help believers. This seeming lack of help and reluctance to demonstrate love in a crisis is often excused by his followers on the grounds that he is sovereign. "God is God, after all," they say, when prayer appears to have fallen on deaf ears.

In contrast, Jesus Christ's power over people is not absolute. While God could exercise complete control, he chooses not to do so. God himself has limited the extent of his own control over us to allow us to have free will. Without it we would be robots who would love him only because we were programmed to do so. Therefore he has excluded himself from being able to force grace onto anyone and everyone who is not necessarily looking for it.

However, the unchanged and true risen Jesus Christ, being the perfect image of the invisible God of love, offers healing to everyone who comes to him for it, just as he did in the New Testament. The often prayed-to out-of-focus version does not.

The pure in heart will see God and the poor in spirit will have the benefits of the kingdom.

What steps must we take to know the difference?
1. Practise discerning between the commonly upheld and out-of-focus image of God and the character of the true risen Lord Jesus Christ.
2. Study his words and works in the Gospels to grow in understanding of his character.

3. Be convinced by that study that God's will is always to restore.

4. Be continually prepared to have our image of God challenged by scripture – learn to allow modern preconceived ideas about his working and thinking to fall away when they do not match by Jesus' words and works in the New Testament.

5. Seek to imitate Jesus' ministry and that of the apostles as closely as possible.

6. Learn the goodness of the kingdom of God and the true value of the cross and how to proclaim it.

7. Do everything you do for the glory of God.

It is God himself who has hidden these secret things of the kingdom from the cynical and the blinkered thinker, and longs to show them to those of us with a child's poverty of spirit and purity of heart. Anyone of us who find it awkward and difficult to receive the kingdom of God, with the simplicity and wholeheartedness of a little child may never walk in its blessings.

So let's do some work to settle down the wings of the theological butterfly in our brains and that cleverest of its fluttering thinking that seems to promise satisfaction of intellect and the justification of work and ministry. Let's throw away, as far as strength will allow, those thoughts that ever doubt his passion for all who suffer.

Let's beg him to fill our poor souls with his Holy Spirit so that our footsteps are guided nearer and nearer to the Christ risen out of the pages of the Gospels and not out of the experience the unbiblical thinking of others. Only then will we begin to demolish those arguments and pretensions that spring up from our life experiences and set themselves up in our minds against the true knowledge of God and the truths of the kingdom, and allow us to take a firm hold of every such thought to make it conform to the character and the will of the Christ of the Gospels, the perfect image of the invisible God.

TRUSTING THE LORD

As we begin to praise the Father and give thanks for something we may not have previously been aware of, the full purposes of Calvary and its role in the journey from Eden to the new Jerusalem, the kingdom comes near and life begins to be restored around us.

As our prayers for others change from pleadings to praising, from interceding to the giving of thankofferings, so the Holy Spirit brings near the kingdom and we increasingly see the Lord fulfilling his words.

The kingdom of God comes near not so much because we request it, but because we expect it.

7

RESTING IN THE KINGDOM

It is not easy for us, in this fearful and anxious world, to calm our souls down enough to actually rest in God in our hearts. We can busily involve ourselves with study and a variety of other things not bad in themselves, and in varying degrees we get some idea about how to witness, encourage and bless other people.

We even know how to think about and analyse all these things, sometimes to the point of thinking we are perfecting them. But to lift our souls up and above the busy traffic of the material world, and what I have called the 'self kingdom', and consciously ponder on the presence and mysteries of God himself? This seems so often to be beyond the reach of our Christian experience.

Yet if only we could in some way grasp the character of God, relating to him as he is, we would enter a kingdom where there is greater immunity from this self-driven world and its consequences. We would be able to receive into our spirits the victory that Christ won for us on the Cross, which is living *in* Jesus Christ. That is what we seek!

This little book is about the deepening of our working relationship with God, so living in Christ and operating in the mind of Christ, in his will, is absolutely essential to that relationship.

IN CHURCH?

We cannot, and should not, be satisfied merely with the tasks we are called upon to perform. Ultimately, we will find out that theological study and church attendance are but forms which will give little satisfaction in and of themselves. All routine activities will have to become the things that the Lord has ordained them to be: means through which we look for and find God.

What I am saying is that we will not find our deepest pleasure in the mechanics of spiritual and ecclesiastical disciplines alone. We find it in the experience of being brought closer to God.

PAUL AND US

Paul's cry in Philippians 3:10 (NIV) was, "I want to know Christ—yes!" It was this desire to know Jesus better and better that produced Paul's leading knowledge of salvation, church order, the deepening of our relationship with God, and evangelism. His deep passion to know God was vital, and of course God gave his servant Paul that heart desire.

God gave him revelation. The Holy Spirit used that servant, the epistles were written. Paul's knowledge was based on his experience with Christ and flowed out of a close relationship with the Lord Jesus, which began when the apostle was converted, the event to which he testified repeatedly and fearlessly. Paul, as he said, was obedient to the heavenly vision. We need to be obedient to the heavenly vision too.

It may be that we have satisfied ourselves not with seeking the face of God, but with studying facts *about* God. Many of us have become satisfied with a religion *about* Christ without the reality of Christ.

THE BIBLE

The Bible, the divinely inspired written Word of God, records God's self-revelation to mankind and includes many accounts of experiences of God's might acts. Historically it is true and factual.

So in one sense it might be said that our theological perspectives have developed out of the personal encounters that our predecessors had with the living God. But true knowledge *about* God is only the first step towards coming into the presence of God and coming under his kingdom rule and authority.

The Bible is also a map to show us the way to relate to God. As Christians, we study and debate the map and, too often, fail to set out on the journey.

LOVE SURPASSES KNOWLEDGE

There is a place, like a fig tree, in the kingdom of God which is far greater than knowledge; it is a simple, yet eternally profound place where we actually abide in Christ's love. This is, indeed, the shelter of the Most High.

Remember the apostle's prayer, that we would each "know the love of Christ, which surpasses knowledge"? Of course knowledge is important, but love "surpasses knowledge". Doctrinal knowledge is the framework, the vehicle, that opens the door to divine realities, but love causes us:

.... to know this love that surpasses knowledge — that you may be filled to the measure of all the fullness of God.

Ephesians 3:19 (NIV)

There is, close at hand, a dwelling place of love which God wishes us to enter. It is a place where our knowledge of God is fulfilled by the substance of God, to overflowing.

May Christ through your faith [actually] dwell (settle down, abide, make his permanent home) in your hearts!

May you be rooted deep in love and founded securely on love, that you may have the power and be strong to apprehend and grasp with all the saints [God's devoted people, the experience of that love] what is the breadth and length and height and depth [of it]; [that you may really come] to know practically, through experience for yourselves] the love of Christ, which far surpasses mere knowledge [without experience]; that you may be filled [through all your being] unto all the fullness of God [may have the richest measure of the divine Presence, and become a body wholly filled and flooded with God himself]!"

Ephesians 3:17–19 (AMP)

As kingdom seekers, is this not our aim, to be rooted deeply in love, to grasp the breadth, length, height and depth of God's love and to know for ourselves the deep, personal love of Christ?

Christian, can any objective be more wonderful? Indeed, to be filled and flooded with the presence of his Holy Spirit, and to dwell in him for ever is the core hope of the gospel! And that in-filling can happen! John affirmed that Jesus would baptise (immerse) in Holy Spirit. When Paul found believers who hadn't been baptised in the Spirit, he saw that was put right (see Acts 19:2). They had repented, they believed in Jesus, there was more they needed, and they received as described in that incident.

GOD EXPERIENCED

God cannot truly be known without also, somehow, being experienced. If we had never seen a sunrise or a starry night sky, could any human description substitute well enough for our own eyes experiencing the expansive and majestic beauty of it all? Awe comes from seeing and encountering, not just from knowing that in theory, somewhere, a beautiful sky exists.

Likewise, to truly know God we must go on seeking him until we pass through the outer, informational realm about God, and actually find for ourselves the living presence of the Lord himself. There is the upward call of God in Christ Jesus. It draws us through the world of our doctrines into the immediacy of the divine presence. The journey leaves us in the place of transcendent surrender, where we listen to his voice and, from listening, climb up into his love.

GOD'S LAST MOVE
The last great move of God in this world will be well signposted by an outpouring from Christ of an irresistible desire in us, his people. To those who really look forward to his reappearing there will come, in ever-increasing waves, substantial seasons of renewal from the presence of the Lord.

> "Repent, then, and turn to God, so that your sins may be wiped out, that times of refreshing may come from the Lord, and that he may send the Messiah, who has been appointed for you—even Jesus. Heaven must receive him until the time comes for God to restore everything, as he promised long ago through his holy prophets."
>
> *Acts 3:19–21* (NIV)

When that time arrives, intimacy with Christ in those who are abiding in him will be restored to its highest level since the days of the early church.

Many outside this move of God, as well as those touched and healed by it, will look and wonder: how did these common people obtain such power?

They will see miracles of the same kind and in the same volume as when Jesus Christ walked the earth. Multitudes will be drawn into the valley of decision for him. For them, truly, the kingdom of God will be close at hand.

WHAT ABOUT ME?
But There will be no mystery about this for those who the Lord has drawn to himself. There will be no mystery about their being empowered this way. Having gone back to the

simplicity and purity of devotion to Christ, they will know him and his love.

STEPPING IN NOW

At the beginning of his ministry, Jesus called to Philip to follow him and he went in search of Nathanael to tell him that he had found the Christ. Nathanael was at first somewhat doubtful, but nevertheless he went along to see.

Noticing Nathanael coming towards him, Jesus remarked, "Here is a true Israelite in whom there is nothing false."

Wondering how this man might happen to know him, Nathanael asked, "How did you know me?"

"When you were under the fig tree I saw you." Jesus told him. (See John 1:48)

Something outside the normal experiences of everyday life must have happened to Nathanael under the fig tree, or the Saviour would not have mentioned this one particular place. Any other place would have done equally as well. Our Lord might have seen him just as easily in his own garden or in the street. But there was something in his answer that was highly significant to Nathanael. In those days there were many devout people looking for the 'consolation of Israel', the coming of the King of the Jews. It is easy to believe that Nathanael was one of those people, sitting under the fig tree, praying like many others for the swift coming of the Messiah.

When Jesus said to him, "When you were under the fig tree, I saw you," Nathanael immediately answered, "You are the Son of God, you are the King of Israel." He was under the tree for this purpose and not once only, but very probably for months and perhaps even for years. He had been praying for this very thing. He had selected one special fig tree to be his place for prayer. Under that particular tree he would have prayed long and often for Israel's King to come. So when Jesus said, "When you were under the fig tree, I saw you," he would have known straight away that his often repeated prayers were answered, thus triggering the response, "Rabbi, you are the Son of God; you are the King of Israel."

It is good for devout folk to have a secret place of communion like this with God; perhaps on a mossy knoll in the woods, under a big old oak tree, on a grassy spot on the bank of a stream, or under a shade tree that grows alongside a river meandering through a meadow. We can retreat there when the shadows of night begin to fall or when the light of the morning streaks across the sky, and there we can pour out our praise and thanksgiving from the fullness of our hearts.

It is a delight to have an altar of prayer in some secluded place. There we meet God and tell him all our sorrows and cares, and we can tell him, too, about his loving kindness. There we can beg his grace to uphold and sustain us through all our difficulties in life, and there we can worship at his feet. Bless his name!

Have we got a "fig-tree"? and are we often found under it?

THE HUMILITY OF BROKENNESS

An outward sign of those who seek the kingdom and walk in its blessings is their humility. This humility is not the kind that manifests itself before and towards other people through a desire to fulfil good works or to 'play a part', it is a naturally outworking virtue springing from deeper harmony with the Lord.

Humility is the bloom and the beauty of holiness. The chief mark of counterfeit holiness is its lack of humility, and true renewal is the building up of the Christian to know what he is, who he is and how to travel through life in the brokenness of our association with the cross.

God has given us this road to our renewal through our experiences of brokenness, in our vulnerability, and through healing deep in all aspects of our life. This holy vulnerability is very close to the idea of sanctified brokenness.

Holy brokenness is not easy to define, but can be seen

quite clearly in the reactions of Jesus as he approached the cross. Supremely, we see it in his crucifixion.

Living in the kingdom of God, growing in the mind of Christ, doing the will of God, sometimes leads to even our own Christian brothers and sisters not understanding.

At such times, we might recall that Jesus' brethren were not entirely faithful at his point of brokenness. Think of Peter's denial!

If we can bow our heads, simply continuing to obey God and to accept his will despite the misunderstandings around us, then we begin to approach this idea of holy brokenness.

When we are misrepresented or deliberately misinterpreted, we remember that Jesus was falsely accused and yet he held his peace. Recalling this, we are released from the need to attempt to justify ourselves.

When another person is preferred to us, and we are deliberately passed over, we may remember that the crowd cried, "Away with this man and release unto us Barabbas." Jesus knew what it meant to be rejected by other people. He knows what it is like for us.

Sometimes, our plans are brushed aside by our leaders, or perhaps we see the work of years brought to dust by what appears to be someone else's ambition. We remember that Jesus allowed men to lead him away to crucify him, and he accepted that place of apparent failure. He was not made bitter by the injustice. For Jesus, insults, rejection and the cross just provided more opportunities for love and the release of forgiveness.

When, in order to be in the right place with God in a particular set of circumstances it is necessary to take the humbling path of confession and restitution, remember that Jesus, who was without sin, made himself of no reputation and humbled himself unto death, even death on the cross. Then we, who do sin, can bow our heads in holy brokenness.

When others behave badly towards us, we do well to remember that when he was crucified Jesus prayed, "Father forgive them, for they know not what they are doing."

The readiness to forgive can be very hard and can take a lifetime to get to grips with. But, if we can bow our heads and accept that any bad behaviour towards us is being permitted (though not willed) by our heavenly Father, then this is brokenness.

How hard it may be sometimes, but we must apply in our own hearts and minds this scripture:

> And we know that in all things God works for the good of those who love him, who have been called according to his purpose.
>
> *Romans 8:28* (NIV)

When people expect the impossible of us, perhaps more than time or human strength can give, remember that Jesus said, "This is my body which is given for you."

If we can repent of our self-indulgence and lack of self-giving to others, then we begin to understand the power of this brokenness. It is not that there is anything romantic or wonderful about being wounded, or experiencing chaos in this life. Through holy brokenness, through experiencing life beyond the far edges of comfort and through seeking the kingdom, the wounded discover his love for us.

Wounds are painful. They leave scars, which may be dead, tender, hard, beautiful, fascinating, terrifying, pathetic. These scars can easily distort the meaning of life and our perception of reality.

The Holy Spirit comes to mend all, and sometimes, with our scars, we can all rejoice in what they tell us. When we see his healed scars, we are reminded of God's wonderful healing work in us. Then, like countless other Christians who have run the race faithfully, we, too, can walk and work with Jesus in his kingdom.

8

HIDING IN HIM

We need to find practical ways of pouring ourselves (or asking the Holy Spirit to pour us) over the sometimes seemingly impassable boundaries and barriers between the kingdom of God and the kingdom of self. How do we find a way of dwelling more naturally within the kingdom of God? Here's a helpful analogy, one way to help us to think about such things:

THE SPORT OF TRIPLE JUMPING
The reader may know the Triple Jump by a different name; the Hop, Skip and Jump. Tracing its origins back to the ancient Olympics, it's a track and field athletic sport, in many ways like the Long Jump, but involving a "hop, skip and jump" routine.

The competitor sprints down the track. Then he or she performs a hop, a step and then a jump into the sand pit. The first phase requires the athlete to jump off one foot. The second is to land on the same foot and jump again. The third time the jumper lands on the other foot and jumps onwards into the sand pit.

Nobody would for one moment consider these three stages of the event to be individual sporting activities in their own right – we see them as the three parts of a whole. They flow together as one movement. Once the run has started, the three steps follow each other automatically. And that's how we might perceive the importance of Jesus' showing us how to die, rise and shine, finishing up being hidden with him in God.

FROM THE NEW TESTAMENT
The Gospels tell us about Jesus arriving, working, and going home again, by way of the cross and being raised from the dead. Paul then picks up the message and tells us what it should all mean to us.

Here is where I find it helpful to think of my personal journey using my picture of 'triple jumping'. There seem to be two hurdles for us to work our way over. First we should clarify some of our understandings of Baptism as Paul taught it, and Pentecost as Jesus taught it. And if we try this journey from their (Paul's and Jesus') point of view we may begin to arrive somewhere that may feel very different, and very exciting.

BAPTISM
It is easy to understand Baptism as itself being the beginning of a new life, but Paul also teaches it as being a death. The church sometimes teaches Pentecost as the church's birth date and/or as being a divine injection of power into the human being, but Jesus taught it as something nearer the completion of God's process of atonement. So let's set out on a really radical adventure and see where it leads us.

DISCIPLES LEARN AND FOLLOW
Perhaps if we are truly to follow Jesus then we might think about following where he went; Crucifixion, Resurrection and Ascension, his 'triple jump', his three steps back into heaven.

THREE STEPS TO HEAVEN

STEP 1 CRUCIFIXION

This is not likely to happen to us, physically! But Paul saw it, in our case, as killing off the self-nature we inherited from the old man Adam. So it would be good if we can do it. Surely, if we would like to be more holy because he is holy then we would need to see as much of the old nature as possible killed off.

Jesus once talked to Nicodemus about the children of Israel being infested with snakebite in Moses' day. Moses, on God's instruction, put up a stake and nailed a bronze replica snake to it. Gazing upon it they got healed. In the Hebrew scripture, that is the same word used for serpent that described Satan in Eden, the snake that turned the Adam of God's likeness into a mess.

Now the nature of the messed-up Adam lives in all of us. Can we get him killed off? Well, Paul is absolutely clear on this. Crucifixion of the old Adam in us is not something we can go out and organise for ourselves – it happened by the grace of the Holy spirit at our baptism. The process of our being crucified has begun. Paul says in Romans 6 (NIV): "Or don't you know that all of us who were baptized into Christ Jesus were baptized into his death?"

We might not have felt anything quite so painful at our own baptism other than the shock of cold water, but it surely happened. If today we still come across what feels like bits of the enemy hanging around inside us, we must rest assured that these are only memories and temptations deep inside.

ENTER THE ENEMY!

We should, however, be well aware of the enemy's strategy in all these thoughts. He comes and whispers suggestions of evil in our ears and minds, various and differing aspects of Adam's fallen nature – potential doubts, blasphemies, jealousies, envying and pride. He then turns round and says to us: "Oh, how nasty you must be to even think of things like this! It's very obvious that you are not being a good Christian, because if you were it would have been impossible for these things to have got into your heart!"

The soul often goes on to accept this premise as being true becaus this reasoning sounds so very plausible. The soul then comes under condemnation straight away, and is filled with discouragement. At this point it is easy for Satan to lead us on from there into actual sin.

For this reason one of the most fatal things in the life of faith is discouragement. One of the most helpful is holy cheerfulness. We should have joy in knowing that the beast in us is dead!

STEP 2 RESURRECTION

The church teaches us that resurrection will happen to us after death and when Jesus returns. Not until then?

Again, Paul is most clear on this. When we are baptised we are immersed in Christ's death. Our messy Adam bits are killed with him. Our old serpent is merged with Jesus on the cross. The old Adam dies as well.

Baptism is about new life, of course it is, but we must start by appreciating it as death.

And Paul teaches that, just because Jesus was risen afterwards so we are risen as well It's automatic.

> "...having been buried with him in baptism, in which you were also raised with him through your faith in the working of God, who raised him from the dead."
>
> *Colossians 2:12* (NIV)

ANOTHER ANALOGY

We start off on our journey of growing in holiness like a hollow mould figurine filled with wax that, when the molten wax was originally poured in, filled every nook and cranny on the inside, right down to the tips of the toenails. The figurine looks exactly like us but it is filled with the soul and spirit of the old Adam, of fallen man.

Our baptism, our crucifixion, our ongoing sacrifice of ourselves, does not kill the figurine itself but begins and continues with the process of digging out all the wax inside.

Resurrection then follows and refills it with the new Adam, Jesus. Galatians 2:20 helps us to understand:

> "I have been crucified with Christ and I no longer live, but Christ lives in me. The life I live in the body, I live by faith in the Son of God, who loved me and gave himself for me."

Praying for an ongoing crucifixion of the old Adam, sanctification day by day, gives God our permission to find wax, dig it out and automatically refill the gaps with the Spirit of Jesus, the Holy Spirit. Thus, bit by bit, we become more Christlike, we attain a little more to having the mind of Christ.

We might then assume that there is only one reason why Christians do not feel like risen people hidden in God with Christ – it's because we are not sufficiently taught or reminded that baptism is, and baptism was, as much a spiritual death as a new life.

So we shared in his crucifixion when we were baptised, and resurrection follows on from that because it happened to him.

The way Paul words these things is to tell us that we were immersed in Christ on the cross and we stayed immersed as he died and were then resurrected, so we get resurrected with him!

STEP 3 ASCENSION

The ascension of Jesus was a unique, once for all event, marking the conclusion of our Lord's series of appearances to the apostles in his resurrection body.

What happened to the first generation of Christians was that they were immersed in Holy Spirit, first at Pentecost and then by going on being filled. Believers not yet present on the day of Pentecost could be baptised (immersed) in the Holy Spirit on other occasions down the ages ever since, and can be today. So we might think of Pentecost (and subsequent in-filling by the Holy Spirit) as being our third step.

WHAT DID JESUS SAY?

We must look at Pentecost through the words of Jesus. Many of us have been taught that the church's annual celebration of Pentecost is simply the birthday of the church. Many others of us are taught about Pentecost as an infilling with Holy Spirit power from on high. To gain a full understanding of the meaning, we do need to think about how Jesus defined Pentecost in this way, recorded in John 14:15–21 (NIV):

> "If you love me, keep my commands. And I will ask the Father, and he will give you another advocate to help you and be with you forever—the Spirit of truth. The world cannot accept him, because it neither sees him nor knows him. But you know him, for he lives with you and will be in you.
>
> "I will not leave you as orphans; I will come to you. Before long, the world will not see me anymore, but you will see me. Because I live, you also will live.
>
> "On that day you will realize that I am in my Father, and you are in me, and I am in you.
>
> "Whoever has my commands and keeps them is the one who loves me. The one who loves me will be loved by my Father, and I too will love them and show myself to them."

'On that day' is a direct reference to Pentecost. Jesus teaches his disciples that the real value of Pentecost is that we will at last 'get it' subcutaneously (really) and know his living in us and our living in him. On that day the Spirit came and caused them to live *in* Jesus, and with him and through him, spiritually and literally. We can't see Jesus now as he is in heaven. But through Pentecost we can be hidden in God with Christ as well! Colossians 3:1–4 (NIV) says:

> Since, then, you have been raised with Christ, set your hearts on things above, where Christ is seated at the right hand of God.
>
> Set your minds on things above, not on earthly things. For you died, and your life is now hidden with Christ in God. When Christ, who is your life, appears, then you also will appear with him in glory.

Set your minds on things above, not on earthly things? Here again is the call to move away from the self kingdom and to seek the kingdom of God.

Hidden in God with Christ? Here is yet another analogy! Imagine slicing an apple exactly in half and looking at the cut face of the fruit. Imagine we can see two seeds in the core, one represents Christ and the other represents ourselves. Imagine living like this all day long, immersed in God with our Saviour and soaked continuously in the juice of the Spirit!

This scripture extract from Paul we can now understand much more fully. He says that we should set our minds on things above. If we are really there, permanently soaked in the apple core in our analogy, then we should be seeing kingdom things, as Jesus did!

And as for telling us that we shall appear with him in glory, we have extreme joy in knowing that 'glory' is a commonly used biblical word for the *Shekinah*. We look forward to the day when Jesus, the light of the world, returns in glory, in the dazzling array of the *Shekinah*. We want to be immersed with him inside it.

BACK TO PENTECOST

Now let's go back to the record of Pentecost. When the Holy Spirit came, the effects were amazing. Those people didn't get the odd word of knowledge or the encouragement to go on a prophecy seminar, or see some act of healing now and again! Immediately their whole personalities changed. It was as though heaven 'opened' around them!

They changed from being scared, hiding disciples with little talent into the most extraordinary people, who saw the world as Jesus saw it, and ministered to the world in continuation of Jesus' ministry.

After the disappointment of his crucifixion, after the joy of seeing him resurrected, after the sadness of watching him go in his ascension, now they would have understood that he had come back for them in the Spirit. They were reunited. They had at last begun to know the mind of Christ. He had come to draw them up into himself in new life, hidden with him.

Because they had learned from Jesus, they now understood that they had moved into partnership with him. They had largely moved from the self-kingdom to living and having their being in the kingdom of God.

Then, turning outward and back towards the world around them, they would have really understood what Jesus meant when he told them, "As the Father sent me, now I am sending you." He had been in that heavenly place with the Father since eternity and had come to be in the world, from that place of intimacy. Now, as a result of Pentecost, the disciples were lifted into this intimacy and were being sent out on a mission, in obedience to the Great Commission.

We need constant reminding of the true meaning of Pentecost and how to follow the three steps to kingdom living. The cares of the world are constantly rubbing out this image from in front of our eyes. Here are two ways to make sure we are constantly reminded of these facts:

REMINDERS
• Remember the apple – an apple cut in half, with the cut face pointing towards us. There are two seeds. You and Jesus, hidden in God with him. Note: apple seeds are all potential apple trees. Not all will grow into magnificent fruit trees but, for the time being, they are where they are, soaking in the apple's juices, Think: hidden in God with Christ.

• Remember the Eucharist. We can remember his sacrifice for us. So let's get to doing that, not just going through a procedure because that's what our church does sometimes. When we get to take the bread and the wine we give thanks for all God's gifts in creation and redemption, and, as we receive, we can also give thanks for the Holy Spirit, his immersing of us, his empowering of us to go on doing all that Jesus calls us to do. This should affect all that we do and say.

My picture of triple jumping might simply help us to remember Jesus' crucifixion, resurrection and ascension. It may also help us to remember that on our journey on the Way we are to crucify our old sinful flesh and to walk *in* Christ in the eternal life that is only found in him; and that we are to go on in the way the Spirit is leading us, until we are at last in the heavenly presence of our Lord and King, Jesus – for ever.

SHOULD THIS BE ONGOING?
Paul wrote this:

> For we who are alive are always being given over to death for Jesus' sake, so that his life may be revealed in our mortal body.
>
> *2 Corinthians 4:11* (NIV)

9

NETWORKING WITH GOD

JESUS' WORKING RELATIONSHIP WITH THE FATHER

We could say that God opened the gates of Eden again, to win people for his new creation – back from the reckless, damaging and self-destructing kingdom of self that we have turned this world, and ourselves, into. To do this he has sent us his Son, Jesus.

Jesus, both true man and true God, temporarily surrendered his majesty in heaven so that he could become flesh. This way he can touch our human lives from every angle.

THE BIGGER PICTURE

At this point we could again look at the record of his three years in mission, detail by detail, wondering which particular item to emphasise out of a wealth of God's wisdom, but in doing it we might miss the overall picture. If we stand back from it all, and view it from a wider angle, we can see that his mission included these three fascinating aspects: he taught about the kingdom of God, he healed people in droves, and he taught us to pray. There is obviously so much more and the chief focus, as we have already shown, is his death for our sins and his having been raised to life on the third day.

But for the moment let us look again at the three aspects of healing, teaching and prayer. The true disciple's driving aim is to imitate Jesus and to learn as a disciple about the kingdom of God, receiving and believing and practising what our Lord taught about it so that we can live the life of the kingdom: working, teaching, preaching, healing and praying.

GOD'S WISDOM
The new creation, which began with the firstfruit of the resurrection of Jesus, has begun. As people are born again by the Spirit of God, they come into the kingdom. The new heaven and new earth will be much better than this present situation. In it there will be neither sin nor suffering, for every tear will have been wiped away. Such a new creation is hard for us to imagine as we are used to living in a world which in so many ways operates in opposition to the Creator.

Wisdom, the practical application of the word of God, will be given to us by the Holy Spirit if we ask. When we speak of the wisdom of God himself, we have in mind all that he is going to do to bring to fulfilment his purposes. In his wisdom, he has chosen to work in and through us to achieve his purposes. So every Christian disciple must be a close imitator of Jesus. We must preach, heal and pray as we have been taught in God's Word to do.

KINGDOM LIVING
We could speak of *kingdom living* or *life in the kingdom*. What we have in mind is the outpouring of heaven down onto this earth, together with all the kingdom duties, riches and benefits.

THEME OF THINGS
The overall theme that we have learned in this small book seems very clear; the kingdom of God is God's place of restoration, body, mind and spirit. We were out of it through Adam's disobedience but grace (an undeserved gift) has won the day for us. The gateway through is open, and is a person – Jesus. He has come to rescue us.

WHERE ARE WE IN THIS?
The Gospels contain something else of overriding kingdom interest: they show how ordinary Christians can become disciples working in tandem with Jesus, willing labourers in that restoring operation, changing the world around us from the sick and sorry place it has become, into somewhere much more like Eden. Surely that must ring a bell in every Christian heart – surely every disciple longs to see the world around them changed?

PROJECT SKILLS AND TALENTS
In order to do this, two things are needed to force a way through for the kingdom: *authority* to overcome evil and the *power* to move it out of the way.

Proclaiming the kingdom, and healing the sick and performing other miracles, Jesus emphatically demonstrates that he has both these tools of power and authority, and he exercises them. What we know is that they were clearly manifested from the moment when the Spirit was clearly seen to come upon Jesus by the Jordan. When we are immersed in the Holy Spirit, then we know an empowering and a new authority which is maintained as we operate in line with the mandate we have been given by the Lord.

That is very interesting – it means that we too, as his disciples under his gentle yoke, can work with authority and power in his kingdom.

Many today are experiencing the baptism of the Holy Spirit. That it is essential is shown so clearly in Acts 19:2 when the apostle Paul asked "Did you receive the Spirit when you first believed?" The question would not have made sense if it were automatic! And many are earning the necessity of going on being filled with the Spirit, as the New Testament instructs.

That being the case, there is something more we can also learn and receive as we look at Jesus' life of prayer. What we want to learn from Jesus is how he maintained that prayer life on earth: Jesus the man connecting with God the Father. The Father affirmed him publicly as the Spirit appeared like a dove. The Father, we have seen and heard, is well-pleased with Jesus his Son. And the Spirit is poured out. So we are to be in the Son, living in him, and him working in us, the Spirit empowering us to do the work of Jesus on earth, under his kingdom authority.

WORKING TOGETHER

Jesus' way of praying seems to have been utterly different from the kinds of prayer practised by the religious professionals of his day. Here was a rabbi (teacher) with a difference! There could be no better way for us to learn to continue his kingdom ministry on earth than to study his prayer habits – a habit being an act which we repeat so often that we do not need to make a fresh decision to do it each time it is done. It just happens. Jesus loved to pray; sometimes praying even became his way of taking a rest; he prayed so often that it became a natural part of his life, like breathing in and out.

WE CAN PRAY

We have a tendency to believe in the potential importance of the way in which we do things in our Christian life. The way in which we might minister to others does not, however, significantly affect the quality of the fruit we look for from that ministry.

For the Christian disciple to gain in kingdom authority and kingdom power there is nothing we need more than to learn to live a life of prayer, bearing in mind that there are two ways of receiving instruction on how something should be done: one of them is by being told how to do something; the other one is by watching someone else actually doing it.

The second of these is the more practical method, and the easier one. The best way to learn how to pray is to watch Jesus praying, and then try to imitate him. This is not quite the same as studying the things he said about prayer, worthwhile though that might be, or even how he took on board other people's prayer requests, but how Jesus himself prayed, often surrounded by the same circumstances and temptations that we have to face up to in our own lives.

EXAMPLES

In our search for God's wisdom in this, we can find the best instruction on how to organise our prayer lives from two sections of the Bible: the Gospels and the Psalms. In very general terms, the Gospels show us the outward side of Jesus' prayer habits, while certain Psalms reveal glimpses of what might have been going on inside.

There are fifteen different references in the four Gospels that reveal Jesus' praying, Matthew talks about three of them, Mark and John have four each, while Luke, with eleven of these allusions, fills in most of the picture for us. The Gospels make it quite clear that Jesus was used to praying; he prayed often; he needed to pray, and he loved prayer.

SAME BATTLEFIELD

Sent into the world as was Jesus, with the same aims and objectives, into the same battlefield with the same enemy to fight, and with exactly the same Holy Spirit to gift and encourage us, when will we discover that this authority and power that we need to make changes around us comes to us through our keeping in close contact with the source, and with appropriate insulation from this power-draining world we live in?

We shall pass quickly through those fifteen references of the Gospel writers, keeping them in their chronological order.

• The first reference is in Luke, in his third chapter. The first three Gospels all speak about Jesus' double baptism, but it is Luke who pops in the words, "and as he was praying…" It was while he was waiting in an attitude of prayer that

Jesus received the gift of the Holy Spirit. He was not about to launch out on his public ministry without the promised anointing he would have looked forward to from the ancient writings. And now, standing in the river Jordan, he waits and prays until the sky above is torn by the glowing gleams of glory-light from heaven. The dove-like Spirit comes down on him and remains with him. Prayer brings power.

The time and place for praying is the time and place of power. I find it helpful to think of prayer is being like screwing down tightly the terminals that connect us to the divine source, so that authority and power can flow freely without any loss or break in the circuit.

• The second reference for us to think about is in Mark 1:35.

Jesus had spent the day before in his adopted hometown, Capernaum, and it had been an extraordinarily busy one for him. He taught in the synagogue service, was interrupted by a demon-possessed man, casting it out, and then was nearly thrown down a cliff. After all that there was the healing of Peter's mother-in-law, and then as the sun went down, the great crowd of diseased and demonised filled the narrow street outside the house until long after dark, while he went up and down the queues, touching and healing them all. It must have been an exhausting day's work.

After a day like that any one of us would need to go to bed early and have a long lie-in the following morning, but Jesus seems to have another way of recovery, other than sleeping. He has a way of slipping off early in the morning to some quiet place or other where he can be on his own to converse with his heavenly Father.

A few of his disciples, with Peter in the lead, start out to look for him, with some degree of urgency because a queue is already forming outside Peter's house again and filling the street. They find him in the hills at prayer, and try to persuade him to go back with them. The crowds were gathering again and looking for him, but Jesus knows his mission.

This is a real temptation for any disciple today. It would have been so much easier to go back down the hill with them and do kingdom business again with the same people as before. He would know where he was with them. He would have learned their beliefs and their doubts. As those who preach the kingdom today know only too well, it is always much more difficult to go somewhere new to meet unknown people with their unknown levels of scepticism.

But now there is no thinking to be done about it, no doubt in his mind about what he should do. We should not be surprised by this, nor envy his clarity of thinking. Prayer clears our view of things up ahead; it steadies our nerves; it stiffens our resolve and strengthens the spirit. The more busy the day ahead threatens to be, the more important it is for the kingdom disciple, like Jesus, to keep a morning rendezvous with the Father.

• Our third reference is in Luke 5, perhaps on the trip suggested just now in Jesus' reply to Peter about moving on, in one of those numerous Galilean villages along the way. Jesus has healed someone in the advanced stages of leprosy who has then gone out and ignored his express instruction, widely publishing the fact of his miraculous healing. As a result, there are now enormous crowds blocking Jesus' way through the village and the place can no longer contain the crush. He sets off for the countryside, where there should be more space, and the people could now collect more comfortably around him.

HE WITHDRAWS

Jesus often withdrew to lonely places and prayed. This occasion does not suggest a one-off act of praying, but rather a habit of praying that runs across several days or even weeks. Being forced by the sheer size of the crowds to go into the country areas, and being consantly under pressure there from people demanding kingdom restoration from sickness,

Jesus has much less opportunity to get away on his own, and needs it more. So while he patiently carries on with his work among them, he determinedly looks for any occasion to step back from the crowds in order to spend a time in prayer. This is not today's common routine of going off to work in some act of ministry or other first, and then saying a little prayer to bless it or to bless the people around us.

But the priority must first be given to prayer. Then we find that the works growing out of that prayer are charged with surprising power. It is in prayer alone that we become more sensitive to the macro and micro decisions and directions of God.

The tighter the tension, the more time there should be for unhurried prayer. This is a hard lesson but a fabulous investment!

• Our fourth note about prayer is found in Luke 6:12. This is probably somewhere around the middle of the second year of Christ's public ministry. He has been having what to us would be the most exasperating experiences with some of the national leaders from Judea who followed him everywhere, criticising and nagging, sowing seeds of doubt into his child-minded, spiritual Galileans. This is also the evening before he appointed the men who were to be the leaders of Christianity after his leaving, and preaching the mountain sermon.

Luke does not suggest that Jesus decided in advance to spend the whole night in prayer. It is more likely he was wearied in his spirit by the non-stop nit-picking and demonic hatred of these stalkers; thinking about the seriousness of the work that needed doing the next day, and there is only one thing for him to do. He knows where to find rest and relaxation, fellowship with his Father and his calming influence and wise advice.

Unhurried prayer

A PICTURE OF JESUS AT PRAYER
As he prayed and listened and spoke with God, daylight faded into twilight, and that gave way to a thousand brilliant stars spraying their sparkling light across the heavens and down to where he was. Still he prayed, while both the blue above him and the darkness around him deepened. The peace of the Father must have brought an ever deeper calm.

Feeling quite at home in the world of the Father's loving presence, he would have become completely unaware of passing time, praying on and on, until eventually the grey streaks of dawn crept up over the face of the land of Israel, perfumed by the heavy dews of an eastern night, and Jesus would be warmed by the rays of a new day's sun.

Then he called his disciples together and chose twelve from them. He turned to the gathering crowds and power flowed out of him and healed them all. Is it any wonder, after a night like that!

POTENTIAL
What would the church be like today, if all our frustrations and embarrassments were followed by, and all our decisions and public statements preceded by, nights of unhurried prayer? What power would pour through us, too, in our relationship with God?

• We can find our fifth mention of prayer in Matthew 14 and Mark 6 with John hinting at it in his own chapter 6. It is around the time of the third Passover in Jesus' ministry, the beginning of his last year of service. They have been kept extremely busy with huge crowds coming and going. The shocking news of John the Baptist's death at Herod's hand has reached them. They need to rest, to step back awhile in peace and quiet, and get back into proportion the antagonism rapidly building up against them.

With this aim in mind they take a boat and head towards the eastern shore of the lake, but the enthusiastic gathering of people wait and watch to see the direction they are going in and, spreading the news, literally run around the head of the lake and get to their destination before they do.

The disciples step out of the boat for a much needed break and straight into a huge company, thousands of them, waiting for Jesus.

Did a little sense of impatience break out among the disciples, frustrated that they were not to be allowed a little time off? But Jesus was "moved with compassion" and, tired though he might well have been, he patiently spent the whole day teaching them.

In the evening the disciples suggested sending them away to get something to eat, but Jesus, with a handful of bread and fish, satisfied their hunger.

WHAT ABUNDANCE!

Nothing has appealed down the centuries to the masses in every land like the ability to provide plenty to eat. Tens of thousands of people go to sleep hungry every night.

So, not surprisingly, someone then suggested a great popular uprising under this wonderful man's leadership, to throw off the oppressive Roman yoke. If only he would agree, it would be tremendously successful, or so they think.

With the sheer power of his presence felt so obviously at certain times, he calmed down the movement and told the disciples to sail back before him to the other side of the lake while he sent the crowds home.

And what did he do then? He went up on the mountain to pray, and stayed there until the morning. A second night spent in prayer! Time on his own to pray was his one invariable offset to all mission difficulties, all temptations, and all his needs. How much more there must have been in his prayers than we would know today!

THE NEED DEEPENS

The remaining prayer incidents on our list occur when Jesus was in the last year of his earthly ministry, and the religious leaders' attitude to him was hardening ever further. The dreadful shadow of the cross was growing darker and deeper across his path. The spiteful hatred of the opposition was deepening. The struggle of the crowds, and the disciples, to understand him grew more noticeable.

Significant numbers of his followers began to fall away. He would spend more time with the Twelve. He made frequent visits to farther points on the border of the non-Jewish world. The inevitable events of the cross to come were now never far from his thoughts.

• It is against this background that we find the sixth mention, in Luke 9, when they were up north in the vicinity of the Roman city of Caesarea Philippi. Jesus was alone, as far as the crowds were aware, but he seemed to be drawing the Twelve much more into his inner life.

Some of these later quoted incidents of prayer seem to suggest that Jesus is teaching the disciples the same love for prayer that he had himself. Well, they were going to need to pray a great deal in the years to come without his physical presence. It is easy to suspect as well that he was longing for a closer relationship with them. He loved human fellowship, as Peter, James, John, and Mary, Martha and many others would have known full well.

• The seventh mention of Jesus at prayer is further on in this same ninth chapter of Luke, and talks about yet a third whole night of prayer. Matthew and Mark write about the transfiguration scene as well, but it is here in Luke that we can see him going up into the mountain to pray, and that it was during that time of prayer that his appearance began changing. Rather than study the Transfiguration, we can hold on to the significant point that it was while he was praying that it happened at all!

• Our next example is in Luke 10. Jesus has organised a group of missionary men, sending them on in twos ahead of him to towns and villages. They came back to him with excited reports of the authority and power which had accompanied their work. Standing with them chattering all around him, his heart overflowing with joy at their enthusiasm, he looked up to heaven and poured his heart out to his Father.

AWARENESS
Jesus seemed to be constantly aware of the Father's presence, and the most natural thing in the world was talking to him. They were always within speaking range of each other, and always on speaking terms.

• Moving on to the ninth example at the beginning of Luke11, which is very much the same idea as our sixth example, we can read that, "One day Jesus was praying in a certain place. When he finished, one of his disciples said to him, "Lord, teach us to pray, just as John taught his disciples."

Doubtless these disciples were men of prayer. Jesus had already talked to them quite a bit about prayer, but it was looking as though they had begun to notice at last what a large part prayer had to play in his life and ministry. And they had been watching some of the marvellous results. They must have been quite impacted, through all this, that there must be some as yet unexplored attraction, and power, in prayer, which they really should find out about. Their request must have thrilled him! At last they were waking up to the great secret of power and that the first step in learning how to pray is to pray: "Lord, teach me to pray!"

NETWORKING WITH GOD

• The next time we find Jesus praying is in John 11:41, 42. A large group of people had been gathering outside the village of Bethany, around a tomb where the body of a young man had been buried four days earlier. Among them was Mary, still crying after four days, and Martha, trying to be more composed, their personal friends, and the villagers, and some people from Jerusalem.

After some family hesitation, the stone across the mouth of the tomb was rolled aside on Jesus' say-so. It seemed as though he had been praying about raising Lazarus from the dead before coming to the tomb, and the successful outcome that followed was in answer to his prayer. How evident it becomes as we go on through these quotes that all the fantastic power displayed during his short career on this earth came through prayer.

PRAYER POWER

The greatest power that God has entrusted to us is prayer-power and we are left wondering how many of us fail that trust, while this extraordinary power that is put into our hands (under the lordship of Jesus) lies so unused!

So here he was in front of the tomb with the dead body inside. To all intents and purposes trust is blind, except it can see upwards. Real trust cannot see impossibilities and cannot hear doubt. It only listens to God and only sees his will and goes with it.

Trust has little to do with believing that God *can* do something but everything to do with knowing that he *will*. Trust like this only comes from close and continuous contact with God.

It is given birth in the secret places of the heart at prayer. It takes time to grow, time to feed on the open Word, with sharp ears and a quiet and reverent soul.

We find our eleventh mention in John:12:27–29 (NIV). A few days before Jesus' arrest a group of Greek visitors, in the city for Passover, asked to have an interview with him.

Pleased to grant their wish, Jesus' thoughts were immediately overtaken by an ink-black shadow of the cross coming so close now. He must have shrunk in horror, internally, from the knowledge of what he was facing, knowing the inevitability but realising God the Father's will for us that will come into reality through his dying. He prayed,

> "Now my soul is troubled, and what shall I say? 'Father, save me from this hour'? No, it was for this very reason I came to this hour. Father, glorify your name!"
>
> Then a voice came from heaven, "I have glorified it, and will glorify it again."
>
> The crowd that was there and heard it said it had thundered; others said an angel had spoken to him."

NEARNESS

As soon as the prayer was away from his lips, the audible voice of God answered him, "I have glorified it, and will glorify it again."

Think of this – how close heaven must be to us! How quickly the Father hears when we pray! We might only imagine that he is bending over, concentrating, listening intently, keen to pick up even the softest of our whispered prayers as he did when he searched for Adam and Eve in the garden of Eden.

The folks standing around Jesus at this moment, whose ears were full of earthly noises, quite unused to being tuned to a heavenly voice, heard no words at all. But Jesus had something very precious here – he had a trained ear. We can discover how he might have got it by reading Isaiah;

> "The Sovereign Lord has given me a well-instructed tongue, to know the word that sustains the weary. He wakens me morning by morning, wakens my ear to listen like one being instructed.
>
> The Sovereign Lord has opened my ears...."

I have not been rebellious....

Isaiah 50:4–5 (NIV)

A taught ear is even more essential to prayer than a taught tongue, and this daily routine morning appointment with God seems fundamental to getting both of them.

• The next example is recorded for us in Luke:22. It is Thursday night of Passion week; Jesus and the disciples are upstairs in the room in Jerusalem where they are celebrating the old Passover feast and, while they are at it, he is instigating the new memorial one. But even the atmosphere of that holy evening is tainted and ruffled by the disciples' self-seeking arguments. He graciously corrects them and then talks to Peter, and using his old name, he tells him:

> "Simon, Simon, Satan has asked to sift you as wheat. But I have prayed for you, Simon, that your faith may not fail. And when you have turned back, strengthen your brothers."

INTERCESSION

This is so exciting – he had been praying for Peter by name! Praying for other people was one of his prayer habits. And he is still doing just that. His never ending occupation, now that he is seated at the Father's right hand in heaven, is praying for each one of us who trust him. By name!

• We cannot really study John 17, our thirteenth example of Jesus' prayer, in the narrow confines of such a small book as it is too great a passage. We can only fit it in as we go along. These prayers come from the standpoint of someone who is thinking of his work down in the world as already finished, although the climax on the cross has not happened yet. Now Jesus is talking in terms of coming back into his Father's presence, to be reinstated in glory with him.

- The next mention of prayer we come to brings us into the grounds of Gethsemane garden, a favourite prayer spot, frequently visited by Jesus when he was in Jerusalem. The record of this prayer incident is found in Matthew 26, Mark 14 and Luke 21. It is a little later on that same Thursday evening, after the talk in the upper room, when Jesus leads the little group of disciples out of the city gate to the east, across the fast flowing muddy Kidron and into the enclosed grove of olive trees on the far side.

He would not be able to sleep that night – within an hour or two the armed soldiers and the Jewish mob, led by the traitor, would be in the very same garden looking for him, and he intended to spend the available time in prayer.

The Spirit drew him on his own still further into the moonlit recesses of the garden, and there a great soul struggle ensued. It looks like a renewal of the same conflict he experienced in John 12 when the Greeks came to talk to him, but perhaps a great deal fiercer.

He was now beginning to realise in his spirit that he was about to be made sin for us and the awful realisation of it came in on him with such terrific reality that it seems as if his physical frame could not bear the mental agony. What could it possibly have felt like for unfallen, sinless man to face an encounter with the sin of the whole world which was going to kill him?

Our thoughts follow the lonely figure among the trees, straightaway kneeling, now falling on the ground on his face, praying that if it would be possible such a desperate thing would pass him by. Our ears catch a snatch of that prayer: "Abba, Father, all things are possible for you. Take this cup from Me; yet not my will but yours."

And the flickering flare of torches in the distance, between the trees, tells him that the moment is here.

- Lastly, three of the seven sentences he speaks on the cross are prayers. Even while the soldiers are hammering in the nails he thinks of us, "Father, forgive them, they know not what they do."

After hanging silently for three hours, he sobs loudly the piercing, heart-rending cry, "My God, My God, why have you forsaken Me?" A little later the triumphant shout proclaims his work to be done, and then his very last word is a quietly breathed prayer, "Father, into your hands I commend My spirit."

RESORTING TO PRAYER

How much his praying meant to Jesus! It was not merely a regular habit, but his resort in every emergency, however serious or slight it was. When hard pressed by his work, he prayed. When needing support in fellowship he found it in prayer. He chose his disciples and received his messages on his knees. If tempted, he prayed; if criticised, he prayed. When he became tired in body or in spirit, he had recourse to prayer.

Prayer brought him almost unbelievable power at the beginning, and it kept flowing. Prayer is the main arterial road down which come all the supplies of authority and power needed by God's people to share in Jesus' ruling of the kingdom and to change the world with him.

It is only in prayer that we can find the way to move closer to God, the source and destination of our whole existence. But at the same time we have to realise that the closer we come to him the stronger are likely to be his demands that we let go of the many 'safe' structures we have built up around ourselves.

In summing up this little book, prayer is such a radical act because it demands of us that we criticise our whole way of being in the world, lay down our old selves and accept our new self which is, in a nutshell, Christ.

Prayer, then, is the act of dying to everything we think of as being our own, and of being born to a new life which is not of this world. It is the kingdom of God.

He himself bore our sins in his body on the tree, so that we might die to sins and live for righteousness; by his wounds you have been healed.

1 Peter 2:24 (NIV)

SUMMARY

This whole world, whatever the context in which the reader perceives it, is divided into two kingdoms. These are the one ruled by God and the one ruled by self.

The call of scripture is for us to cease living in one and seek to live in the other. To make the assumption, whatever our justification, that we already live wholly in the kingdom of God is a dangerous self-deception. If we say we have no sin we deceive only ourselves!

Most of us spend a high degree of our time living in the kingdom of self. To deny such a thing is to swim in pools of spiritual pride that have no place in the kingdom of God. Neither can this be measured simply by examining ourselves for signs of sins but by having the humility to admit that we all have a long way to go to reach the state that God requires of us.

We cannot reach any place of satisfaction with this uncomfortable thought purely through commitment, church attendance or through Baptism, by water and/or by Spirit, by a constant refilling of that Spirit or by the ease of use of his gifts.

However spiritual we believe we might be, however biblically correct our lives might be, the only real place for the spiritual Christian is 'face-down in humility' before the cross of Christ. We must seek entry into the kingdom of God through its work, time and time again, longing to be made more holy so that Christ's yoke is an easier and more comfortable fit on our backs. It is a lifetime's devotion.

We were chosen and appointed to bear fruit, something we can only do by dwelling in obedience. But we must always be recognising that our thoughts are not his thoughts, always regretting it, always seeking his work in us to bring us nearer to being, like the unfallen Adam, people who might look for a moment as if we really were made in his image after all!

Our hope is that this way we grow and move in increasing harmony with God's walking and God's working in this world, not necessarily only to make the world a 'better' place but to see it turned into a place that greatly glorifies him through our Lord Jesus.

This is the way the kingdom grows, this is our part in its growing.

Books by Mike Endicott include:

God and Me
Rediscovering Kingdom Healing
The Passion to Heal

A full list of books and booklets in print may be found at:

www.jacobswell.org.uk
www.simplyhealing.org

ebook editions are also available

The Order of Jacob's Well Trust
Forge House, Clomendy Rd, Old Cwmbran, Wales NP44 3LS UK

www.ingramcontent.com/pod-product-compliance
Lightning Source LLC
LaVergne TN
LVHW012332180725
816574LV00032B/740